Pasa el Examen de Ciudadanía Americana

3ra edición

LEARNING EXPRESS ®

NEW YORK

D1209393

Copyright © 2008 LearningExpress, LLC.

Library of Congress Cataloging-in-Publication Data:
Pass the U.S. citizenship exam. Spanish
Pasa el examen de ciudadanía americana.—3ra ed.
    p.   cm.
ISBN: 978-1-57685-618-5
    1. Citizenship—United States—Examinations—Study guides.   I. LearningExpress
(Organization).   II. Title.
JK1758.M3718   2008
323.6'230973—dc22

                                                                2008000909

Printed in the United States of America

9 8 7 6 5 4 3 2 1

Third Edition

ISBN: 978-1-57685-618-5

For information on LearningExpress, other LearningExpress products, or bulk sales, please write to us at:
    LearningExpress
    55 Broadway
    8th Floor
    New York, NY 10006

Or visit us at:
    www.learnatest.com

CONTENIDO

CÓMO USAR
ESTE LIBRO

Este libro te ayudará a aprobar el examen de ciudadanía estadounidense y también te mostrará los otros pasos que seguir para obtener esta ciudadanía. Puedes estudiar este libro por tu cuenta, con un compañero de estudios o en una clase regular.

Atención: Este libro no ofrece consejos legales. Para asesoría legal, consulta a un abogado de inmigración.

✪ Lo que encontrarás en este libro

El Capítulo 1 muestra los beneficios y los problemas posibles de llegar a ser ciudadano estadounidense. Tienes que saber por qué quieres ser ciudadano de los Estados Unidos ya que el Servicio de Ciudadanía e Inmigración (USCIS) te pedirá que expliques tus razones.

El Capítulo 2 te explica los pasos que tienes que seguir para convertirte en ciudadano. Recuerda que las leyes de naturalización pueden cambiar. Consulta a tu abogado o a un representante del USCIS para obtener la información más reciente.

El Capítulo 3 contiene la lista de las oficinas regionales del USCIS donde puedes obtener información o enviar tu solicitud ya completa del formulario N-400.

El Capítulo 4 es el más largo del libro. Tiene 23 lecciones sobre la historia de los Estados Unidos y sobre su sistema de gobierno. Al principio de cada lección encontrarás una lista de palabras en inglés con sus definiciones y su traducción al español que tendrás que aprender. La página siguiente de cada lección empieza con una lista de preguntas del examen del USCIS que tendrás que memorizar. Una vez que hayas memorizado estas preguntas y sus respuestas y que hayas estudiado la información al comienzo de cada lección, haz los ejercicios que las siguen para asegurarte que hayas aprendido bien la lección. Las respuestas correctas se encuentran en la última página de cada lección. Evita mirar las respuestas antes de haber respondido por tu propia cuenta a todas las preguntas.

Durante el examen el agente del USCIS dirá una frase en voz alta que tú tendrás que escribir. Al final de cada lección encontrarás una práctica de este dictado. Además podrás practicar la entrevista; primero deberás practicar leyendo ejemplos de preguntas y respuestas de este tipo de entrevistas. Luego podrás responder con tus propias palabras. El dictado y la entrevista se llevarán a cabo en inglés.

El Capítulo 5 es una lista de todas las palabras claves de las 23 lecciones del Capítulo 4. Estas palabras en inglés están ordenadas alfabéticamente y junto a ellas se encuentran sus definiciones en inglés y sus significados en español. Esto te servirá como diccionario si tienes problemas mientras te preparas para el examen.

El Capítulo 6 es una lista de 100 preguntas oficiales que pueden aparecer en el examen del USCIS. Estas preguntas y respuestas son de las lecciones del Capítulo 4 y están ordenadas por tema. Lee este capítulo cuando quieras revisar las preguntas sobre la historia oficial de los Estados Unidos.

El Capítulo 7 te mostrará muchos ejemplos de preguntas y respuestas del formulario N-400 "Solicitud para Naturalización". Éstas son preguntas que los funcionarios del USCIS pueden hacer el día de tu entrevista. Hay preguntas que se forman de distintas maneras pero que tienen la misma respuesta. Piensa cómo contestar a cada pregunta antes de ver las respuestas posibles. Todas estas preguntas y respuestas de ejemplo corresponden al Capítulo 4.

El Capítulo 8 tiene todas las oraciones de dictados del Capítulo 4. Puedes practicar estas oraciones llenando los espacios vacíos de la página opuesta.

El Apéndice A contiene la lista actualizada con teléfonos y direcciones de todas las oficinas del USCIS en los Estados Unidos, donde puedes solicitar y entregar los formularios N-400, así como recibir información y asesoría sobre todos los procesos de naturalización. Además, contiene la lista con dirección y teléfonos de todas las embajadas de los países que sostienen relaciones con los Estados Unidos.

El Apéndice B consta de una lista de organizaciones dedicadas a ayudar a inmigrantes que te recomendamos que contactes si requieres asistencia.

El Apéndice C es un ejemplo del formulario N-400 que tendrás que llenar para solicitar la nacionalidad.

Pasa el Examen de Ciudadanía Americana

☆ Pass the U.S. Citizenship Exam ☆

CAPÍTULO 1

¿Quieres ser ciudadano?

Hay muchas razones por las cuales la gente quiere convertirse en ciudadanos estadounidenses. Como también hay otras tantas por las que muchas se niegan a hacerlo. Piensa por qué quieres llegar a ser ciudadano de los Estados Unidos. A través del libro, los términos siguientes se usarán indistintamente: "U.S." y "Estados Unidos". Un ciudadano "americano" es lo mismo que un ciudadano estadounidense.

✪ Razones por ser ciudadano

Aquí se encuentran algunos beneficios de convertirse en ciudadano estadounidense. Considera qué significa cada beneficio. Pon una marca al lado de las razones por las que tú quieres convertirte en ciudadano estadounidense.

_____ tener derecho de votar en las elecciones.

_____ poderte postular a un cargo público.

_____ poder solicitar empleo con el gobierno.

_____ poder solicitar que tus familiares inmediatos vengan a los Estados Unidos.

_____ para que los miembros de tu familia puedan venir a los Estados Unidos rápidamente.

_____ para que tus hijos solteros puedan solicitar la ciudadanía.

_____ poder obtener beneficios del seguro social (_Social Security_) incluso si vives en otro país.

_____ poder vivir fuera de los Estados Unidos sin miedo de perder tu ciudadanía.

_____ poder viajar con un pasaporte estadounidense.

_____ poder reingresar a los Estados Unidos más fácilmente.

_____ no tener que renovar tu tarjeta de residencia, o _Green Card_.

_____ no tener que notificar en caso de un cambio de domicilio.

_____ no ser deportado.

_____ obtener más beneficios del gobierno.

_____ no tener que preocuparte por las nuevas leyes migratorias.

✪ ✪ ✪

ALGUNAS DE LAS RESPONSABILIDADES DE UN CIUDADANO

El juramento de afiliación que vas a tomar para hacerte ciudadano incluye solamente algunas de las responsabilidades de un ciudadano estadounidense. Otras responsabilidades son

▸ Participación en el proceso político por medio del registro para votar y votar en las elecciones.
▸ Servir como jurado.
▸ Mostrar tolerancia hacia las diferentes opiniones, culturas, religiones y grupos étnicos que se encuentran en los Estados Unidos.

✪ ✪ ✪

✪ Razones para no convertirse en ciudadano

_____ tener que tomar un juramento de obediencia a los Estados Unidos.

_____ la posibilidad de tener que dejar de servir a tu país natal.

_____ poder perder tu ciudadanía en tu país de origen.

_____ poder perder tus propiedades y posesiones en tu país de origen.

_____ poder perder el derecho de votar en tu país de origen.

_____ tener que pasar un examen sobre la historia y el sistema de gobierno de los Estados Unidos.

_____ poder ser deportado si se descubre que has mentido en tu solicitud de ciudadanía.

_____ la posibilidad de que se te pueda negar la ciudadanía si se descubre que has mentido para obtener tu residencia permanente en los Estados Unidos.

Ahora, observa cuántas opciones has marcado. Si hay más de la primera lista, muy bien. Si has marcado más razones de la segunda, tal vez te conviene pensar más en este proceso antes de continuar.

Para mucha gente, las razones para convertirse en ciudadano estadounidense son más grandes que las razones para no hacerlo. Piensa en por qué quieres ser ciudadano estadounidense USCIS. Es posible que necesites responder a esta misma pregunta en tu entrevista con el USCIS:

✪ ✪ ✪

¿Por qué quieres convertirte en ciudadano de los Estados Unidos?
Why do you want to become a United States citizen?

✪ ✪ ✪

CAPÍTULO 2

El proceso para convertirte en ciudadano

Este capítulo te demostrará cómo llegar a ser ciudadano estadounidense. Hay muchos pasos que seguir. Es posible que nesesites algunos meses para completar todas las etapas. Lee este capítulo con cuidado, para que no cometas el error de omitir ningún paso.

✪ ¿Estás listo?

Encierra en un círculo **Sí** o **No.** Si puedes contestar que **Sí** a todas las preguntas, entonces quiere decir que estás listo para solicitar la ciudadanía estadounidense.

Sí   **No**   ¿Tienes por lo menos 18 años de edad?

Sí   **No**   ¿Has sido residente legal y permanente de los Estados Unidos por cinco (5) años o más, o has estado casado(a) por tres años al menos con alguien que sea ciudadano(a) desde hace por lo menos tres años?

Sí   **No**   ¿Has estado físicamente presente en los Estados Unidos por lo menos dos años y medio ($2\frac{1}{2}$), o medio ($\frac{1}{2}$) año si estás casado(a) con un(a) ciudadano(a) de los Estados Unidos?

Sí   No   ¿Has vivido en el mismo estado o distrito en los tres (3) últimos meses?

Sí   No   ¿Estás dispuesto(a) a jurar obediencia a los Estados Unidos?

Sí   No   ¿Tienes una conducta moral?

Sí   No   ¿Puedes leer, escribir y hablar un inglés básico?

Sí   No   ¿Tienes conocimiento de la historia y el gobierno de los Estados Unidos?

Si has contestado **Sí** a todas las preguntas anteriores, estás listo para solicitar la ciudadanía americana. Si has contestado **No** a algunas de las preguntas anteriores, consulta con un especialista de inmigración. Hay muchas razones para responder **No** que no te impiden que solicites tu ciudadanía.

El formulario N-400 contiene unas cuantas preguntas sobre asuntos criminales y de tu pasado criminal. Siempre debes contestar estas preguntas honrada y claramente. Si se encuentra que has mentido en tu solicitud, tu petición por ciudadanía será negada, incluso si el delito mismo no fuera impedimento para que te hagas ciudadano. Siempre sé honrado, tanto en la solicitud como en la entrevista.

✪ La solicitud

Necesitas enviar una solicitud llamada N-400 *Application for Naturalization* al USCIS. (Nota: es posible llenar tu solicitud N-400 tres meses antes de haber cumplido los cinco años como residente permanente.) También tienes que enviar dos fotos de tamaño pasaporte y un cheque (o un *money order* de un banco estadounidense) por el costo de la solicitud más un cargo por la investigación de huellas digitales (cuando este libro fue impreso, el precio de la solicitud era de $595 y el precio por la investigación de las huellas digitales de $80). Estos costos pueden ser pagados en un solo cheque (total de $675). Suscribe el cheque a nombre del *United States Citizenship and Immigration Services.*

LO QUE TIENES QUE ENVIAR AL USCIS:

▸ **Formulario N-400 (haz una copia para ti antes de enviar la solicitud original por correo)**

▸ **Dos fotos de tamaño pasaporte**

  ▸ **Estas fotografías se deben tomar de $\frac{3}{4}$ en fondo blanco impresas en papel fotográfico.**

  ▸ **No podrán tener una antiguedad mayor a 30 días antes de ser enviadas al USCIS.**

  Escribe con un lápiz tu nombre completo y tu número de residente permanente en la parte trasera de las fotos. Esto no es un requisito, sino una sugerencia en caso de que tus fotos sean separadas de su solicitud.

▸ **Un cheque (o un *money order* de un banco estadounidense) por $675**

  Puedes obtener el formulario de solicitud N-400 en la oficina del USCIS más cercana. Ve la lista del Capítulo 3 para información sobre las oficinas del USCIS. Después puedes tomar uno de los pasos siguientes:

  1. **Una carta para solicitar el formulario.**
  2. **Ir a la oficina y recogerlo personalmente.**
  3. **Llamar por teléfono y pedirles que te envíen el formulario.**

▸ **Visita www.uscis.gov/files/form/N-400.pdf.**

★ ★ ★

También puedes obtener el formulario de solicitud N-400 llamando al teléfono 1-800-870-3676. Sé honrado cuando llenes el formulario de solicitud. Pide ayuda si la requieres. Ve el Capítulo 3 para información sobre dónde obtener esta clase de ayuda.

✪ Huellas digitales

No envíes una carta o tarjeta con tus huellas digitales junto con la solicitud. Después de que el USCIS reciba tu solicitud, te enviarán una carta con la información del lugar más cerca de tu residencia donde te pueden tomar las huellas digitales. Sigue las instrucciones de la carta. El día de tu cita, lleva contigo esta carta, tu tarjeta de residencia permanente y una forma más de identificación personal con fotografía —por ejemplo, licencia de conducir o pasaporte. Tus huellas digitales serán enviadas al FBI para verificar datos sobre tu pasado criminal. Si tienes más de 75 años de edad a la hora de hacer esta solicitud, no se requerirá que te tomen las huellas digitales.

✪ Estudiar

Lee y estudia este libro y cualquier otro material que te ayude a comprender la historia y el sistema de gobierno de los Estados Unidos. Necesitarás saber todo acerca de este libro. Quizás sea útil que tomes una clase que te enseñe cómo pasar el examen de ciudadanía estadounidense.

✪ La prueba

El USCIS tendrá que evaluar tu inglés y tu conocimiento del gobierno y el civismo estadounidense. Tendrás que demostrar que puedes leer, escribir y hablar un inglés básico.

Durante la entrevista, el USCIS te dará un examen acerca de la historia de los Estados Unidos y su gobierno. Te harán preguntas en inglés y tendrás que responder en voz alta y en inglés. Para aprobar el examen tienes que responder correctamente a 70% de las preguntas. Es posible que te den los resultados de tu examen inmediatamente o por correo dentro de los dos meses siguientes. Si no apruebas el examen, puedes tener una segunda oportunidad. Si no apruebas en esta segunda oportunidad, tendrás que comenzar el proceso de nuevo.

Si tienes más de 50 años y has vivido como residente permanente y legal en los Estados Unidos por 20 años, no tienes que tomar el examen de inglés y podrás tomar el examen de civismo en español.

> **Si tienes más de 55 años y has vivido como residente permanente y legal en los Estados Unidos por 15 años, no tienes que tomar el examen de inglés y podrás tomar el examen de civismo en español.**

> **Si tienes más de 65 años y has vivido como residente permanente y legal en los Estados Unidos por 20 años, no tienes que**

tomar el examen de inglés. Podrás tomar una versión más fácil del examen de civismo en español.

✪ ✪ ✪

✪ La entrevista

Después de llenar la solicitud, recibirás una carta que especifica la fecha de tu entrevista. No te asombres si te dan tu cita para dentro de 10 o 12 meses. Esta notificación puede incluir una petición de documentos adicionales que tendrás que llevar en el día de tu entrevista. Si tienes que cambiar la fecha de tu entrevista, comunícate con tu oficina correspondiente del USCIS y explícales la razón para cambiar la fecha. No te olvides que esto puede durar unos cuantos meses. En la entrevista, tendrás que tomar un juramento y prometer que vas a decir la verdad. Te harán preguntas de tu formulario de solicitud N-400. También te harán preguntas personales sobre tus hijos, tu trabajo y tu vida personal. Tendrás que contestar estas preguntas en inglés. Si tienes un problema físico o mental, o invalidez, te pueden eximir de tomar la parte de inglés y civismo del examen. (Nota: En la ceremonia de juramento, tienes que estar dispuesto y preparado a tomar el juramento de afiliación a los Estados Unidos. Si no puedes entender o tomar el juramento debido a un desahucio, no podrás ser elegible para obtener la ciudadanía.)

✪ ✪ ✪

Asegúrate de que cada vez que cambies de dirección notifiques al USCIS. Recibirás solamente una carta notificándote de la fecha de tu entrevista. Si pierdes esa cita sin haber contactado USCIS, tu caso será "*administratively closed*" (administrativamente cerrado) y necesitarás "abrirlo" de nuevo.

✪ ✪ ✪

✪ La a ceremonia de juramento

Si sales bien en el examen y la entrevista, recibirás una carta en aproximadamente dos meses que te dirá la fecha y hora de la ceremonia de tu juramento. En la ceremonia, tomarás el juramento de obediencia (*Oath of Allegiance*). Prometerás ser leal a los Estados Unidos y cambiarás tu tarjeta de Residencia Permanente por un certificado de ciudadanía de los Estados Unidos. Después de esta ceremonia, ¡serás ciudadano!

✪ ✪ ✪

No es sino hasta que tomes tu juramento que te conviertes en ciudadano estadounidense. Abajo encontrarás una traducción aproximada de ese juramento.

✪

JURAMENTO DE AFILIACIÓN

Yo declaro, bajo juramento,

Que absoluta y enteramente renuncio y rechazo toda afiliación y fidelidad a cualquier príncipe, potentado, nación o reino extranjero de quien o del cual yo, antes de hoy, he sido súbdito o ciudadano;

Que voy a apoyar y defender la Constitución y las leyes de los Estados Unidos de América en contra de todo enemigo, ya sea éste foráneo o doméstico;

Que llevaré la buena fe y afiliación al mismo;

Que portaré armas a favor de los Estados Unidos cuando la ley así lo requiera;

Que daré servicio militar en tiempo a las Fuerzas Armadas de los Estados Unidos cuando la ley así lo requiera.

Que voy a desempeñar trabajos de importancia nacional bajo la dirección civil cuando la ley así lo requiera; y

Que tomo esta obligación libremente, sin ninguna reserva mental o propósito de evasión; Entonces

Que Dios me ayude.

✪ ✪ ✪

CAPÍTULO 3

Cómo obtener ayuda

Para llegar a ser ciudadano estadounidense puedes encontrar ayuda en muchos lugares. Este capítulo incluye información de contacto de las cuatro oficinas regionales regiones de los Servicios Americanos de Ciudadanía e Inmigración (USCIS) para que puedas obtener ayuda en la región donde vives.

✪ Información sobre las oficinas del USCIS

Hay cuatro oficinas regionales del USCIS. Busca tu estado y envía tu solicitud a la dirección correspondiente. También puedes contactar la oficina del USCIS para más información sobre el proceso de naturalización.

✪ Norte

Si vives en los estados de

Alaska	Michigan	Oregon
Colorado	Minnesota	South Dakota
Idaho	Missouri	Utah
Illinois	Montana	Washington

Indiana	Nebraska	Wisconsin
Iowa	North Dakota	Wyoming
Kansas	Ohio	

Envía el formulario de solicitud N-400 completo a esta dirección:

United States Citizenship and Immigration Service
Nebraska Service Center
Attention N-400 Unit
P.O. Box 87400
Lincoln, NE 68501-7400
Phone: 402-437-5218

✪ Oeste

Si vives en los estados o territorios de

Arizona
California
Commonwealth of the Northern Mariana Islands
Hawaii
Nevada
Territory of Guam

Envía el formulario de solicitud N-400 llenado a esta dirección:

United States Citizenship and Immigration Service
California Service Center
Attention N-400 Unit
P.O. Box 10400
Laguna Niguel, CA 92607-0400
Phone: 949-360-2769

✪ Sur

Si vives en los estados de

| Alabama | Louisiana | South Carolina |
| Arkansas | Mississippi | Tennessee |

Florida	New Mexico	Texas
Georgia	North Carolina	
Kentucky	Oklahoma	

Envía el formulario de solicitud N-400 llenado a esta dirección:

United States Citizenship and Immigration Service
Texas Service Center
Attention N-400 Unit
P.O. Box 851204
Mesquite, TX 75185-1204
Phone: 214-381-1423

✪ Este

Si vives en los estados o territorios de

Commonwealth of Puerto Rico	New Hampshire	Vermont
Connecticut	New Jersey	Virginia
Delaware	New York	Washington, D.C.
Maine	Pennsylvania	West Virginia
Maryland	Rhode Island	
Massachusetts	U.S. Virgin Islands	

Envía el formulario de solicitud N-400 completo a esta dirección:

United States Citizenship and Immigration Service
Vermont Service Center
Attention N-400 Unit
75 Lower Weldon Street
St. Albans, VT 05479-0001
802-527-3160

✪ Ayuda legal

Si quieres, puedes contratar a un abogado para que te ayude a llenar el formulario de solicitud N-400. Busca en la guía telefónica a la *Bar Association* o *Legal Aid Society*. Muchos abogados de inmigración también se anuncian en las "páginas amarillas". Ten mucho cuidado en elegir un abogado. Pregunta a tus amigos o familiares si conocen a un abogabo bueno.

El *American Immigration Lawyers Association* (AILA) es la mejor organización que puedas contactar para solicitar más información. Cuentan con una lista de más de 10,000 abogados que se especializan en la inmigracíon. Los miembros del AILA han representado a miles de familias estadounidenses que han solicitado residencia permanente para sus cónyuges, hijos y otros parientes cercanos para que puedan entrar y residir en los Estados Unidos. Puedes contactar AILA para obtener información sobre abogados de inmigración a

American Immigration Lawyers Association (AILA)
918 F Street, NW
Washington, D.C. 20004
Tel: 202-216-2400
www.aila.org

CAPÍTULO 4

Lecciones de ciudadanía

Cada una de las 23 lecciones en este capítulo te ayudará a salir bien en el examen de ciudadanía. Trabaja lenta y cuidadosamente a través de todas las lecciones, y haz todos los ejercicios de cada lección.

Lesson 1 / Lección 1

Branches of Government / Ramas del gobierno

✪ Words to Know / Palabras claves

branches: separate parts (ramas)

Congress: people who make our laws (la gente que hace nuestras leyes)

✪ About the Branches of Government / Sobre las ramas del gobierno

There are three **branches** of government so that no one branch or person can have too much power. Each **branch** keeps the others from getting too strong. The three **branches** are:

1. executive
   - president
   - vice president
   - cabinet

2. legislative
   - congress

3. judicial
   - supreme court

The **executive branch** carries out the laws, the **legislative branch** makes the laws, and the **judicial branch** explains the laws. A system of **checks and balances** between branches prevents any one branch from becoming too powerful.

En los Estados Unidos hay tres **ramas** del gobierno para que no haya una sola rama o persona con todo el poder. Cada **rama** previene que las otras no se hagan demasiado fuertes. Estas tres **ramas** son:

1. ejecutivo
   - presidente
   - vice presidente
   - gabinete

2. legislativo
   - congreso

3. judicial
   - corte suprema

La **rama ejecutiva** pone en práctica las leyes, **la rama legislativa** hace las leyes y **la rama judicial** explica las leyes. Un sistema de **cheques y balances** previene que una rama de gobierno tenga demasiado poder.

✪ Repetition / Repetición

Repeat these questions and answers out loud. / Repite estas preguntas y respuestas en voz alta.

1. What are the three branches of our government?
executive, legislative, judicial

2. What is the executive branch of our government?
president, vice president, cabinet

3. What is the legislative branch of our government?
Congress

4. What is the judicial branch of our government?
the Supreme Court

5. What system prevents one branch of government from becoming too powerful?
checks and balances

✪ Exercises / Ejercicios

Los ejercicios siguientes han sido diseñados para familiarizarte con el material de esta lección. El verdadero examen de ciudadanía puede ser una opción oral.

Multiple-choice questions / Preguntas de opción múltiple
The following exercises have been designed to familiarize you with the material of this lesson. The actual citizenship test may be oral or written. / Marca las respuestas a las preguntas siguientes. Las respuestas a estos ejercicios se encuentran en la última página de esta lección.

1. ⓐ ⓑ ⓒ ⓓ   **4.** ⓐ ⓑ ⓒ ⓓ

2. ⓐ ⓑ ⓒ ⓓ   **5.** ⓐ ⓑ ⓒ ⓓ

3. ⓐ ⓑ ⓒ ⓓ

1. What is the executive branch?
   a. Congress
   b. the Supreme Court
   c. president, vice president, cabinet
   d. the president

2. What is the legislative branch?
   a. the Supreme Court
   b. Congress
   c. the cabinet
   d. judicial

3. What is the judicial branch?
   a. Congress
   b. Supreme Court
   c. president, vice president, cabinet
   d. judicial

4. What are the three branches of our government?
   a. congress, president, cabinet
   b. executive, judicial, legislative
   c. president, vice president, cabinet
   d. executive, president, Congress

5. How many branches are there in the government?
   a. two
   b. three
   c. five
   d. fifty

Circle the correct answer / Encierra en un círculo la respuesta correcta.

1. What is the judicial branch?
Congress   Supreme Court

2. How many branches of government are there?
five   three

3. What is the executive branch?
Supreme Court   president, cabinet, vice president

4. What is the legislative branch?
Congress   president

5. What are the three branches of government?
executive, judicial, legislative   federal, state, judicial

"Yes" or "no" questions / Preguntas de "sí" o "no"

Yes   No   The president is in the judicial branch of government.

Yes   No   The Supreme Court is in the legislative branch of government.

Yes   No   There are three branches of government.

Yes   No   Congress is in the executive branch of government.

Yes   No   The president is in the executive branch of government.

Yes   No   There are five branches of government.

✪ Dictation Practice / Práctica de dictado

Write each sentence twice. The first time, copy it. The second time, don't look at it. Have someone read it aloud while you write it. / Escribe cada oración dos veces. La primera vez, cópiala. La segunda vez, haz que alguien lea la oración mientras la escribes.

1. I am a student.

2. I study citizenship.

3. I want to be an American citizen.

1. _____ .

1. _____ .

2. _____ .

2. _____ .

3. _____ .

3. _____ .

✪ Lesson 1 Answers / Respuestas de la Lección 1

Multiple-choice questions / Preguntas de opción múltiple
1. c. president, vice president, cabinet
2. b. Congress
3. c. Supreme Court
4. b. executive, judicial, legislative
5. b. three

Circle the correct answer / Encierra en un círculo la respuesta correcta.

1. What is the judicial branch?
   Congress   (Supreme Court)

2. How many branches of government are there?
   five   (three)

3. What is the executive branch?
   Supreme Court   (president, cabinet, vice president)

4. What is the legislative branch?
   (Congress)   president

5. What are the three branches of government?
   (executive, judicial, legislative)   federal, state, judicial

"Yes" or "no" questions / Preguntas de "sí" o "no"

Yes   (No)   The president is in the judicial branch of government.

(Yes)   No   The Supreme Court is in the judicial branch of government.

(Yes)   No   There are three branches of government.

Yes   (No)   Congress is in the executive branch of government.

(Yes)   No   The president is in the executive branch of government.

Yes   (No)   There are five branches of government.

Lesson 2 / Lección 2

The Legislative Branch / La rama legislativa

✪ Words to Know / Palabras claves

Capitol: building where Congress meets (edificio donde se reúne el Congreso)

legislative branch: Congress (Congreso)

✪ About the Legislative Branch / Sobre la rama legislativa

The **legislative branch** of our government consists of Congress. The **job** of Congress is to make laws. Congress includes the Senate and the House of Representatives. Congress meets in the **Capitol** in Washington, D.C. and is elected by the people. Congress has the power to declare war.

- legislative branch
- Congress (meets in Capitol and has power to declare war)
- Senate
- House of Representatives

La **rama legislativa** del gobierno estadounidense incluye al Congreso. La función del Congreso es hacer las leyes. El Congreso incluye el Senado y la Casa de Representantes. El Congreso se reúne en el **Capitolio** en Washington, D.C. y es elegido por la gente (el pueblo). El Congreso tiene el poder de declarar la guerra.

- rama legislativa
- Congreso (se reúne en el Capitolio y tiene poder de declarar la guerra)
- Senado
- Casa de Representantes

✪ Repetition / Repetición

Repeat these questions and answers out loud. / Repite estas preguntas y respuestas en voz alta.

1. Who makes the laws in the United States?
Congress

2. What is Congress?
Senate and House of Representatives

3. What are the duties of Congress?
to make laws

4. Who elects Congress?
the people

5. Where does Congress meet?
Capitol in Washington, D.C.

6. Who has the power to declare war?
Congress

7. What is the U.S. Capitol?
place where Congress meets

✪ Exercises / Ejercicios

Los ejercicios siguientes han sido diseñados para familiarizarte con el material de esta lección. El verdadero examen de ciudadanía puede ser oral o un examen de respuestas múltiples.

Multiple-choice questions / Preguntas de opción múltiple

The following exercises have been designed to familiarize you with the material of this lesson. The actual citizenship test may be oral or written. / Marca las respuestas a las preguntas siguientes. Las respuestas a estos ejercicios se encuentran en la última página de esta lección.

1. ⓐ ⓑ ⓒ ⓓ   5. ⓐ ⓑ ⓒ ⓓ

2. ⓐ ⓑ ⓒ ⓓ   6. ⓐ ⓑ ⓒ ⓓ

3. ⓐ ⓑ ⓒ ⓓ   7. ⓐ ⓑ ⓒ ⓓ

4. ⓐ ⓑ ⓒ ⓓ

1. What does the legislative branch include?
   a. judicial
   b. Supreme Court
   c. president, vice president, cabinet
   d. Congress

2. What does Congress do?
   a. votes on taxes
   b. makes laws
   c. interprets laws
   d. elects the president

3. What are the two parts of Congress?
   a. the Senate and the Capitol
   b. the Senate and Washington, D.C.
   c. the Senate and the House of Representatives
   d. the House of Representatives and the Capitol

4. Where does Congress meet?
  a. in the White House
  b. in the House in New York City
  c. in the House in Philadelphia, Pennsylvania
  d. in the Capitol in Washington, D.C.

5. Who elects Congress?
  a. the Senate
  b. the vice president
  c. the people
  d. the governor of New York

6. What is the United States Capitol?
  a. the place where Congress meets
  b. the president's official residence
  c. the place where the Supreme Court meets
  d. the office of the executive branch

7. Who has the power to declare war?
  a. the president
  b. Congress
  c. the Supreme Court
  d. the vice president

Matching questions / Preguntas para emparejar

Answer each question with the appropriate letter from the right column. / Relaciona cada pregunta con la letra más apropiada de la columna derecha.

____ Who elects Congress?	A. the Capitol in Washington, D.C.
____ Who makes the laws in the United States?	B. to make laws
____ What is Congress?	C. the people
____ What are the duties of Congress?	D. Senate and House of Representatives
____ Where does Congress meet?	E. Congress
____ What does Congress have the power to declare?	F. war

"Yes" or "No" questions / Preguntas de "sí" o "no"

Yes   No   Congress makes the laws in the United States.

Yes   No   The president has the power to declare war.

Yes   No   Congress includes the Senate and the House of Representatives.

Yes   No   The duties of Congress are to please the people.

Yes   No   The duties of Congress are to make laws.

Yes   No   Congress meets in New York City.

Yes   No   Congress has the power to declare war.

✪ Dictation Practice / Práctica de dictado

Write each sentence twice. The first time, copy it. The second time, don't look at it. Have someone read it aloud while you write it. / Escribe cada oración dos veces. La primera vez, cópiala. La segunda vez, haz que alguien lea la oración mientras la escribes.

1. I like living in United States.

2. I want to be an American.

1. _____.

1. _____.

2. _____.

2. _____.

✪ Lesson 2 Answers / Respuestas de la Lección 2

Multiple-choice questions / Preguntas de opción múltiple

1. d. Congress
2. b. makes laws
3. c. Senate and House of Representatives
4. d. in the Capitol in Washington, D.C.
5. c. the people
6. a. the place where Congress meets
7. b. Congress

Matching questions / Preguntas para emparejar

_C_ Who elects Congress?

_E_ Who makes the laws in the United States?

_D_ What is Congress?

_B_ What are the duties of Congress?

_A_ Where does Congress meet?

_F_ What does Congress have the power to declare?

A. the Capitol in Washington, D.C.
B. to make laws
C. the people
D. Senate and House of Representatives
E. Congress
F. war

"Yes" or "no" questions / Preguntas de "sí" o "no"

(Yes)   No   Congress makes the laws in the United States.

Yes   (No)   The president has the power to declare war.

(Yes)   No   Congress includes the Senate and the House of Representatives.

Yes   (No)   The duties of Congress are to please the people.

(Yes)   No   The duties of Congress are to make laws.

Yes   (No)   Congress meets in New York City.

(Yes)   No   Congress has the power to declare war.

Lesson 3 / Lección 3

The Senate / El Senado

✪ Words to Know / Palabras claves

re-elected: voted into office again (reelegido)

senators: people who work in the Senate making laws (senadores)

the union: all the states of United States (todos los estados de los Estados Unidos)

✪ About the Senate / Sobre el Senado

Congress is made up of the Senate and the House of Representatives. The Senate has 100 **senators**. There are 100 **senators** because there are two **senators** from each state in the **union**. There are 50 states in the **union**. Each **senator** is elected for six years. There is no limit to how many times **senators** can be **re-elected**. You should know who the two **senators** are from your state.

El Congreso está compuesto del Senado y de la Casa de Representantes. El Senado tiene 100 **senadores**. Hay dos senadores por cada uno de los cincuenta estados de la **unión**. Hay 50 estados en la **unión**. Cada **senador** es elegido por seis años. No existe ningún número máximo de veces que un **senador** pueda ser **reelegido**. Debes saber quiénes son los **senadores** del estado en que vives.

Congress
- Senate
- House of Representatives

Congreso
- Senado
- Casa de Representantes

Senate
- 100 senators (two from each of the 50 states)

Senado
- 100 senadores (2 por cada uno de los 50 estados)

Senators	**Senadores**
■ Elected for six years	■ Elegidos por seis años
■ No limit on re-election	■ No hay límite de reelección
■ two from each state	■ dos de cada estado

✪ Repetition / Repetición

Repeat these questions and answers out loud. / Repite estas preguntas y respuestas en voz alta.

1. How many senators are there in Congress?
100 (one hundred)

2. Why are there 100 senators in Congress?
two (2) from each state

3. Who are the two senators from your state?
Pregunta a un profesor, o a un familiar, la respuesta correcta

4. How long do we elect each senator?
six (6) years

5. How many times can a senator be re-elected?
no limit

6. Name one of your state's senators.
Answers will vary by location.

✪ Exercises / Ejercicios

Los ejercicios siguientes han sido diseñados para familiarizarte con el material de esta lección. El verdadero examen de ciudadanía puede ser oral o un examen de respuestas múltiples.

Multiple-choice questions / Preguntas de opción múltiple

The following exercises have been designed to familiarize you with the material of this lesson. The actual citizenship test may be oral or written. / Marca las respuestas a las preguntas siguientes. Las respuestas a estos ejercicios se encuentran en la última página de esta lección.

1. ⓐ   ⓑ   ⓒ   ⓓ   **3.** ⓐ   ⓑ   ⓒ   ⓓ

2. ⓐ   ⓑ   ⓒ   ⓓ   **4.** ⓐ   ⓑ   ⓒ   ⓓ

1. Why are there 100 senators in Congress?
   a. there are 100 states in the union
   b. there are two senators from each state
   c. 100 people are needed to declare war
   d. there is no limit to the number of senators from each state

2. How many times can a senator be re-elected?
   a. zero
   b. one
   c. two
   d. no limit

3. How many senators are in Congress?
   a. 50
   b. 100
   c. 101
   d. 200

4. For how many years is a senator elected?
   a. four
   b. five
   c. six
   d. eight

Circle the correct answer / Encierra en un círculo la respuesta correcta.

1. There are _____ senators in Congress.
100   435

2. A senator is elected for _____ years.
six   ten

3. How many times can a senator be re-elected?
no limit   ten

4. There are 100 senators because there are _____ from each state.
two   four

5. The word "union" means _____.
the United States   provinces in Canada

"Yes" or "no" questions / Preguntas de "sí" o "no"

Yes   No   A senator is elected for 100 years.

Yes   No   There are 100 senators because there are two from each state.

Yes   No   There is no limit to how many times a senator can be re-elected.

Yes   No   A senator is elected for six years.

Yes   No   There are 435 senators in Congress.

✪ Dictation Practice / Práctica de dictado

Write each sentence twice. The first time, copy it. The second time, don't look at it. Have someone read it aloud while you write it. / Escribe cada oración dos veces. La primera vez, cópiala. La segunda vez, haz que alguien lea la oración mientras la escribes.

1. I live in California.

2. I live with my family.

3. I live in California with my family.

1. _____.

1. _____.

2. _____.

2. _____.

3. _____.

3. _____.

✪ Lession 3 Answers / Respuestas de la Lección 3

Multiple-choice questions / Preguntas de opción múltiple
1. b. there are two senators from each state
2. d. no limit
3. b. 100
4. c. six

Circle the correct answer / Encierra en un círculo la respuesta correcta.

1. There are _____ senators in Congress.
(100)   435

2. A senator is elected for _____ years.
(six)   ten

3. How many times can a senator be re-elected?
(no limit)   ten

4. There are 100 senators because there are _____ from each state.
(two)   four

5. The word "union" means _____.
(the United States)   provinces in Canada

"Yes" or "no" questions / Preguntas de "sí" o "no"

Yes   (No)   A senator is elected for 100 years.

(Yes)   No   There are 100 senators because there are two from each state.

(Yes)   No   There is no limit to how many times a senator can be re-elected.

(Yes)   No   A senator is elected for six years.

Yes   (No)   There are 435 senators in Congress.

Lesson 4 / Lección 4

The House of Representatives / La Casa de Representantes

✪ Words to Know / Palabras claves

representatives: people who work in the House of Representatives (representantes que hacen leyes)

term: how long someone works in government (duración de trabajo en el gobierno)

✪ About the House of Representatives / Sobre la Casa de Representantes

Congress is made up of the Senate and the House of Representatives. The House of Representatives has 435 **representatives**. If there are many people in a state, they can elect many **representatives**. If there are few people in a state, they can elect only a few **representatives**. Each **representative** is elected for a two-year **term**. There is no limit to how many times **representatives** can be re-elected.

La Casa de Representantes tiene 435 **miembros.** Si un estado está muy poblado, puede elegir muchos **representantes** pero si un estado está poco poblando sólo puede elegir a pocos representantes. Cada **representante** es elegido por un **término** de dos años. No hay ningún límite en cuanto al número de veces que un **representante** pueda ser reelegido.

House of Representatives
- 435 representatives
- elected for two-year terms
- no limit to the number of times they can be re-elected

Casa de Representates
- 435 representantes
- elegidos por el término de dos años
- no hay límite en cuanto al número de veces que éstos puedan ser reelegidos

✪ Repetition / Repetición

Repeat these questions and answers out loud. / Repite estas preguntas y respuestas en voz alta.

1. How many representatives are there in Congress?
435 (four hundred thirty-five)

2. For how long do we elect the representatives?
two (2) years

3. How many times can a representative be re-elected?
no limit

4. How many representatives does each state have?
depends on how many people live in the state

5. Who represents you in the House of Representatives?
Answers will vary by location.

✪ Exercises / Ejercicios

Los ejercicios siguientes han sido diseñados para familiarizarte con el material de esta lección. El verdadero examen de ciudadanía puede ser oral o un examen de respuestas múltiples.

Multiple-choice questions / Preguntas de opción múltiple
The following exercises have been designed to familiarize you with the material of this lesson. The actual citizenship test may be oral or written. / Marca las respuestas a las preguntas siguientes. Las respuestas a estos ejercicios se encuentran en la última página de esta lección.

1. ⓐ   ⓑ   ⓒ   ⓓ   **3.** ⓐ   ⓑ   ⓒ   ⓓ

2. ⓐ   ⓑ   ⓒ   ⓓ   **4.** ⓐ   ⓑ   ⓒ   ⓓ

1. For how long do we elect the representatives?
    a. one year
    b. two years
    c. three years
    d. four years

2. How many times can a representative be re-elected?

    a. zero

    b. one

    c. two

    d. no limit

3. How many representatives are in Congress?

    a. 100

    b. 101

    c. 435

    d. 450

4. How many representatives are there per state?

    a. 2

    b. 5

    c. 50

    d. depends on the population of the state

Circle the correct answer / Encierra en un círculo la respuesta correcta.

1. There are _____ representatives in Congress.

    435   100

2. A representative is elected for _____ years.

    six   two

3. There is _____ to the number of times a representative can be re-elected.

    a limit   no limit

4. If there are many people in a state, they can elect _____ representatives.

    many   two

5. States with larger populations have _____ representatives.

    more   fewer

"Yes" or "no" questions / Preguntas de "sí" o "no"

Yes   No   A representative is elected for a two-year term.

Yes   No   There are 435 representatives because there are two from each state.

Yes   No   There is no limit to how many times a representative can be re-elected.

Yes   No   A representative is elected for two years.

Yes   No   There are 435 representatives in Congress.

✪ Dictation Practice / Práctica de dictado

Write each sentence twice. The first time, copy it. The second time, don't look at it. Have someone read it aloud while you write it. / Escribe cada oración dos veces. La primera vez, cópiala. La segunda vez, haz que alguien lea la oración mientras la escribes.

1. I want to be an American citizen.

2. I want to be a citizen of the United States.

1. _____.

1. _____.

2. _____.

2. _____.

✪ Lesson 4 Answers / Respuestas de la Lección 4

Multiple-choice questions / Preguntas de opción múltiple
 1. b. two years
 2. d. no limit
 3. c. 435
 4. a. depends on the population of the state

Circle the correct answer / Encierra en un círculo la respuesta correcta.

 1. There are _____ representatives in Congress.
   (435)   100

 2. A representative is elected for _____ years.
   six   (two)

 3. There is _____ to the number of times a representative can be re-elected.
   a limit   (no limit)

 4. If there are many people in a state, they can elect _____ representatives.
   (many)   two

 5. States with larger populations have _____ representatives.
   (more)   fewer

"Yes" or "no" questions / Preguntas de "sí" o "no"

(Yes)   No   A representative is elected for a two-year term.

Yes   (No)   There are 435 representatives because there are two from each state.

(Yes)   No   There is no limit to how many times a representative can be re-elected.

(Yes)   No   A representative is elected for two years.

(Yes)   No   There are 435 representatives in Congress.

Review Quiz 1 / Prueba de repaso 1

Mark the answers for each question on this sheet. The correct answers can be found on the last page of the quiz. / Marca las respuestas a las preguntas siguientes. Las respuestas correctas se encuentran en la última página de la prueba de repaso.

1. (a) (b) (c) (d)   **9.** (a) (b) (c) (d)

2. (a) (b) (c) (d)   **10.** (a) (b) (c) (d)

3. (a) (b) (c) (d)   **11.** (a) (b) (c) (d)

4. (a) (b) (c) (d)   **12.** (a) (b) (c) (d)

5. (a) (b) (c) (d)   **13.** (a) (b) (c) (d)

6. (a) (b) (c) (d)   **14.** (a) (b) (c) (d)

7. (a) (b) (c) (d)   **15.** (a) (b) (c) (d)

8. (a) (b) (c) (d)

1. How many branches of the government are there?
   a. one
   b. two
   c. three
   d. four

2. What is the legislative branch?
   a. Congress
   b. the Supreme Court
   c. the president
   d. the Senate

3. What is the judicial branch?
   a. Congress
   b. the president
   c. the vice president
   d. the Supreme Court

4. What is the executive branch?
  a. president, vice president, cabinet
  b. Congress
  c. the Supreme Court
  d. the House of Representatives

5. What are the three branches of government?
  a. Supreme Court, president, Congress
  b. executive, legislative, judicial
  c. Senate, House of Representatives, cabinet
  d. law, federal, Congress

6. Where does Congress meet?
  a. the Supreme Court
  b. the Capitol in Washington, D.C.
  c. New York City
  d. the White House

7. What is Congress?
  a. the president
  b. the Senate and the House of Representatives
  c. the Senate and the Supreme Court
  d. the union

8. Who elects Congress?
  a. Electoral College
  b. president
  c. the senators
  d. the people

9. Who makes the laws in the United States?
  a. the Supreme Court
  b. the president
  c. Congress
  d. the people

10. What is the job of Congress?
   a. to make laws
   b. to enforce laws
   c. to interpret laws
   d. to collect money

11. How many senators come from each state?
   a. two
   b. four
   c. six
   d. seven

12. How many times can a senator be re-elected?
   a. two
   b. four
   c. five
   d. no limit

13. How long do we elect each senator?
   a. two years
   b. three years
   c. four years
   d. six years

14. How many senators are there in Congress?
   a. 100
   b. 435
   c. 600
   d. 50

15. How many representatives are there in Congress?
   a. 100
   b. 435
   c. 600
   d. 50

Review Quiz 1 Answers / Respuestas de la prueba de repaso 1

1. c. three
2. a. Congress
3. d. the Supreme Court
4. a. president, vice president, cabinet
5. b. executive, legislative, judicial
6. b. the Capitol in Washington, D.C.
7. b. the Senate and House of Representatives
8. d. the people
9. c. Congress
10. a. to make laws
11. a. two
12. c. no limit
13. d. six years
14. a. 100
15. b. 435

Lesson 5 / Lección 5

The Judicial Branch / La rama judicial

✪ Words to Know / Palabras claves

appointed: chosen or selected (nombrado)

chief justice: head of the Supreme Court (juez principal)

interpret: to explain (interpretar, explicar)

judicial branch: the part of the government that includes the Supreme Court (rama judicial)

Supreme Court: highest court in the United States (corte suprema)

✪ About the Judicial Branch / Sobre la rama judicial

The **judicial branch** consists of the **Supreme Court**. The job of the **Supreme Court** is to **interpret** the laws. The **Supreme Court** has nine justices and the **chief justice** is John Roberts. The nine justices are **appointed** by the President. The **Supreme Court** is the highest court in the United States. The **Supreme Court** justices can work in this job until they die. The **Supreme Court** justices work in the **Supreme Court** building.

La **rama judicial** consiste en la **Corte Suprema**. La función de la **Corte Suprema** es **interpretar** las leyes y consiste en nueve jueces. El **jefe de justicia** es John Roberts. Los nueve jueces son **nombrados** por el Presidente y pueden ejercer este cargo hasta que mueran. **La Corte Suprema** es la corte más alta de los Estados Unidos. Los jueces de la **Corte Suprema** trabajan en el edificio de la **Corte Suprema**.

Judicial Branch

Supreme Court

- highest court in the United States
- interprets laws
- works in Supreme Court building
- has nine justices
- chief justice is John Roberts
- justices hold this position until they die

Rama judicial

Corte Suprema

- la corte más alta de los Estados Unidos
- interpreta las leyes
- trabajan en el edificio de la Corte Suprema
- tiene nueve jueces
- el juez principal es John Roberts
- los jueces ejercen esta función hasta que mueran

✪ Repetition / Repetición

Repeat these questions and answers out loud. / Repite estas preguntas y respuestas en voz alta.

1. What are the duties of the Supreme Court?
to interpret laws

2. Who is the chief justice of the Supreme Court?
John Roberts

3. Who appoints the Supreme Court justices?
the president

4. How many Supreme Court justices are there?
nine (9)

5. What is the highest court in the United States?
the Supreme Court

✪ Exercises / Ejercicios

Los ejercicios siguientes han sido diseñados para familiarizarte con el material de esta lección. El verdadero examen de ciudadanía puede ser oral o un examen de respuestas múltiples.

Multiple-choice questions / Preguntas de opción múltiple

The following exercises have been designed to familiarize you with the material of this lesson. The actual citizenship test may be oral or written. / Marca las respuestas a las preguntas siguientes. Las respuestas a estos ejercicios se encuentran en la última página de esta lección.

1. ⓐ   ⓑ   ⓒ   ⓓ   **4.** ⓐ   ⓑ   ⓒ   ⓓ

2. ⓐ   ⓑ   ⓒ   ⓓ   **5.** ⓐ   ⓑ   ⓒ   ⓓ

3. ⓐ   ⓑ   ⓒ   ⓓ

1. How many Supreme Court justices are there?
   a. eight
   b. nine
   c. ten
   d. eleven

2. Who appoints the Supreme Court justices?
   a. the people
   b. Congress
   c. the president
   d. the vice president

3. What is the job of the Supreme Court justices?
   a. to make laws
   b. to elect senators
   c. to interpret laws
   d. to entertain the public

4. Who is the chief justice of the Supreme Court?
   a. George W. Bush
   b. Al Gore
   c. Judge Judy
   d. John Roberts

5. What is the highest court in the United States?
   a. the Supreme Court
   b. chief justice
   c. the White House
   d. the Capitol

Circle the correct answer / Encierra en un círculo la respuesta correcta.

1. The _____ selects the Supreme Court justices.
   president   cabinet

2. The duty of the Supreme Court is to _____ laws.
   interpret   make

3. The _____ Court is the highest court in the United States.
   State   Supreme

4. There are _____ justices on the Supreme Court.
   ten   nine

5. _____ is the chief justice of the Supreme Court.
   John Roberts   Richard Cheney

"Yes" or "no" questions / Preguntas de "sí" o "no"

Yes	No	The duty of the Supreme Court is to make laws.
Yes	No	The duty of the Supreme Court is to interpret laws.
Yes	No	There are nine justices on the Supreme Court.
Yes	No	John Roberts is the vice president.
Yes	No	The president appoints the Supreme Court justices.

✪ Dictation Practice / Práctica de dictado

Write each sentence twice. The first time, copy it. The second time, don't look at it. Have someone read it aloud while you write it. / Escribe cada oración dos veces. La primera vez, cópiala. La segunda vez, haz que alguien lea la oración mientras la escribes.

1. I drive to work.

2. I drive my car to work.

3. I like my job.

1. _____.

1. _____.

2. _____.

2. _____.

3. _____.

3. _____.

✪ Lesson 5 Answers / Respuestas de la Lección 5

Multiple-choice questions / Preguntas de opción múltiple
1. b. nine
2. c. the president
3. c. to interpret laws
4. d. John Roberts
5. a. the Supreme Court

Circle the correct answer / Encierra en un círculo la respuesta correcta.

1. The _____ selects the Supreme Court justices.
   (president)   cabinet

2. The duty of the Supreme Court is to _____ laws.
   (interpret)   make

3. The _____ Court is the highest court in the United States.
   State   (Supreme)

4. There are _____ justices on the Supreme Court.
   ten   (nine)

5. _____ is the chief justice of the Supreme Court.
   (John Roberts)   Richard Cheney

"Yes" or "no" questions / Preguntas de "sí" o "no"

Yes   (No)   The duty of the Supreme Court is to make laws.

(Yes)   No   The duty of the Supreme Court is to interpret laws.

(Yes)   No   There are nine justices on the Supreme Court.

Yes   (No)   John Roberts is the vice president.

(Yes)   No   The president appoints the Supreme Court justices.

Lesson 6 / Lección 6

The Executive Branch / La rama ejecutiva

✪ Words to Know / Palabras claves

Electoral College: group who elects the president (grupo que elige al presidente)

executive branch: part of government made up of the president, vice president, and cabinet (rama ejecutiva)

✪ About the Executive Branch / Sobre la rama ejecutiva

The job of the **executive branch** is to enforce the law. It includes the president, vice president, and cabinet. The first president of the United States was George Washington. The president today is George W. Bush, and the vice president is Richard Cheney. The president is elected for a four-year term and is elected by the **Electoral College**.

El trabajo de la **rama ejecutiva** es hacer cumplir la ley. Esta rama consiste en el presidente, vice presidente, y el gabinete. El primer presidente de los Estados Unidos fue George Washington. El presidente actual es George W. Bush, y el vice presidente es Richard Cheney. El presidente es elegido por un período de cuatro años por el **Colegio Electoral.**

Executive Branch
- president
- vice president
- cabinet

President
- elected for four-year term
- elected by Electoral College

Rama ejecutiva
- presidente
- vice presidente
- gabinete

Presidente
- elegido por un término de cuatro años
- elegido por el Colegio Electoral

✪ Repetition / Repetición

Repeat these questions and answers out loud. / Repite estas preguntas y respuestas en voz alta.

1. What is the job of the executive branch?
to enforce the law

2. Who was the first president of the United States?
George Washington

3. Who is the president of the United States today?
George W. Bush

4. Who is the vice president today?
Richard Cheney

5. Who elects the president of the United States?
the Electoral College

6. For how long do we elect the president?
four (4) years

✪ Exercises / Ejercicios

Los ejercicios siguientes han sido diseñados para familiarizarte con el material de esta lección. El verdadero examen de ciudadanía puede ser oral o un examen de respuestas múltiples.

Multiple-choice questions / Preguntas de opción múltiple

The following exercises have been designed to familiarize you with the material of this lesson. The actual citizenship test may be oral or written. / Marca las respuestas a las preguntas siguientes. Las respuestas a estos ejercicios se encuentran en la última página de esta lección.

1. ⓐ ⓑ ⓒ ⓓ   4. ⓐ ⓑ ⓒ ⓓ

2. ⓐ ⓑ ⓒ ⓓ   5. ⓐ ⓑ ⓒ ⓓ

3. ⓐ ⓑ ⓒ ⓓ   6. ⓐ ⓑ ⓒ ⓓ

1. Who elects the president of the United States?
   a. Senate
   b. Congress
   c. Electoral College
   d. cabinet

2. Who was the first president of the United States?
   a. Bill Clinton
   b. John Roberts
   c. Abraham Lincoln
   d. George Washington

3. What is the duty of the executive branch?
   a. to enforce laws
   b. to interpret laws
   c. to declare war
   d. to buy land

4. For how long do we elect the president?
   a. one year
   b. two years
   c. three years
   d. four years

5. Who is the vice president today?
   a. Richard Cheney
   b. Al Gore
   c. John Roberts
   d. George Washington

6. Who runs the executive branch?
   a. the vice president
   b. the chief justice
   c. the president
   d. the mayor

Matching questions / Preguntas para emparejar

Answer each question with the appropriate letter from the right column. / Relaciona cada pregunta con la letra más apropiada de la columna derecha.

____ first president of the United States	A. four years
____ vice president today	B. George W. Bush
____ how long the president is elected	C. Electoral College
____ president today	D. Richard Cheney
____ elects the president	E. George Washington
____ duty of executive branch	F. enforce the law

"Yes" or "no" questions / Preguntas de "sí" o "no"

Yes   No   The duty of the executive branch is to enforce laws.

Yes   No   The duty of the executive branch is to interpret laws.

Yes   No   George Washington was the first president of the United States.

Yes   No   Bill Clinton is the vice president today.

Yes   No   The president is elected by the Electoral College.

Yes   No   The president is elected for four years.

✪ Dictation Practice / Práctica de dictado

Write each sentence twice. The first time, copy it. The second time, don't look at it. Have someone read it aloud while you write it. / Escribe cada oración dos veces. La primera vez, cópiala. La segunda vez, haz que alguien lea la oración mientras la escribes.

1. I take the bus.

2. I take the bus to work.

3. I like to take the bus.

1. _____ .

1. _____ .

2. _____ .

2. _____ .

3. _____ .

3. _____ .

✪ Lesson 6 Answers / Respuestas de la Lección 6

Multiple-choice questions / Preguntas de opción múltiple
1. c. the Electoral College
2. d. George Washington
3. a. to enforce laws
4. d. four years
5. a. Richard Cheney
6. c. the president

Matching questions / Preguntas para emparejar

E first president of the United States   A. four years
D vice president today   B. George W. Bush
A how long the president is elected   C. Electoral College
B president today   D. Richard Cheney
C elects the president   E. George Washington
F duty of executive branch   F. enforce the law

"Yes" or "no" questions / Preguntas de "sí" o "no"

(Yes) No The duty of the executive branch is to enforce laws.

Yes (No) The duty of the executive branch is to interpret laws.

(Yes) No George Washington was the first president of the United States.

Yes (No) Bill Clinton is the vice president today.

(Yes) No The president is elected by the Electoral College.

(Yes) No The president is elected for four years.

Lesson 7 / Lección 7

The Office of the President /
La oficina del presidente

✪ Words to Know / Palabras claves

advises:	gives help to (da consejo)
cabinet:	fourteen (14) people who help the president make decisions (gabinete)
natural-born citizen:	person born in a country (una persona que nace en un país)

✪ About the Office of the President / Sobre la oficina del presidente

The executive branch of the government includes the president, vice president, and cabinet. To become president, you need to:

- be a **natural-born citizen** of the United States.
- be at least 35 (thirty-five) years old.
- have lived in the United States for fourteen years.

The **Cabinet** is a special group of people that **advises** the president. Some members of the cabinet include the secretary of state, the secretary of agriculture, the secretary of defense, and the secretary of the treasury. The president can serve two terms of four years each. If the president dies, the vice president becomes president. If both the president and the vice president die, then the speaker of the House of Representatives becomes president.

La rama ejecutiva del gobierno incluye el presidente, vice presidente, y el gabinete. Para llegar a ser presidente, uno tiene que:

- ser un **ciudadano por nacimiento** en los Estados Unidos.
- tener por lo menos 35 (treinta y cinco) años de edad.
- haber vivido en los Estados Unidos por lo menos catorce años.

El **gabinete** es un grupo especial de personas que **aconsejan** al presidente. Algunos miembros del gabinete incluyen el secretario del estado, el secretario de la agricultura, el secretario de la defensa, y el secretario del tesoro. El presidente puede servir por dos términos. Si el presidente muere, el vice presidente se convierte en presidente. Si el presidente y el vice presidente fallecen, entonces el portavoz de la Casa de Representantes asume el cargo de presidente.

✪ Repetition / Repetición

Repeat these questions and answers out loud. / Repite estas preguntas y respuestas en voz alta.

1. Who becomes president of the United States if the president dies?
vice president

2. How many terms can a president serve?
two (2)

3. Who becomes president of the United States if the president and vice president die?
speaker of the House of Representatives

4. What are the requirements to be president?
natural-born citizen of the United States, 35 (thirty-five) years old, lived in the United States 14 (fourteen) years

5. What special group advises the president?
cabinet

✪ Exercises / Ejercicios

Los ejercicios siguientes han sido diseñados para familiarizarte con el material de esta lección. El verdadero examen de ciudadanía puede ser oral o un examen de respuestas múltiples.

Multiple-choice questions / Preguntas de opción múltiple
The following exercises have been designed to familiarize you with the material of this lesson. The actual citizenship test may be oral or written. / Marca las respuestas a las preguntas siguientes. Las respuestas a estos ejercicios se encuentran en la última página de esta lección.

1. ⓐ ⓑ ⓒ ⓓ   **5.** ⓐ ⓑ ⓒ ⓓ

2. ⓐ ⓑ ⓒ ⓓ   **6.** ⓐ ⓑ ⓒ ⓓ

3. ⓐ ⓑ ⓒ ⓓ   **7.** ⓐ ⓑ ⓒ ⓓ

4. ⓐ ⓑ ⓒ ⓓ

1. A president can serve how many terms?
   a. one
   b. two
   c. three
   d. four

2. For how many years do we elect the president?
   a. two
   b. four
   c. six
   d. ten

3. Who becomes the president if the president dies?
   a. the vice president
   b. the first lady
   c. a cabinet member
   d. the chief justice

4. What special group advises the president?
   a. Congress
   b. Supreme Court
   c. taxpayers
   d. cabinet

5. Who becomes president if both the president and the vice president die?
   a. the spouse of the president
   b. the chief justice of the Supreme Court
   c. the Senate majority leader
   d. the speaker of the House of Representatives

6. What is one requirement to be president?
   a. be born in Europe
   b. be 35 years old
   c. have lived in the United States for five years
   d. speak Latin

7. Which of the following is NOT a member of the cabinet?
   a. the secretary of state
   b. the vice president
   c. the secretary of the treasury
   d. the secretary of defense

Circle the correct answer / Encierra en un círculo la respuesta correcta.

1. What is one requirement to be president?
born in Canada   natural-born citizen of the United States

2. Who becomes president if the president dies?
first lady   vice president

3. What special group advises the president?
congress   cabinet

4. Who becomes president if the president and vice president die?
speaker of the House of Representatives   Congress

5. How many terms can a president serve?
two   three

"Yes" or "no" questions / Preguntas de "sí" o "no"

Yes   No   To become president, you must be a natural-born citizen of the United States.

Yes   No   The cabinet advises the president.

Yes   No   The duty of the executive branch is to enforce laws.

Yes   No   The first lady becomes president if the president dies.

Yes   No   The executive branch of the government includes the president, vice president, and cabinet.

Yes   No   The president can serve two terms in office.

Yes   No   To become president, you must be at least 50 years old.

✪ Dictation Practice / Práctica de dictado

Write each sentence twice. The first time, copy it. The second time, don't look at it. Have someone read it aloud while you write it. / Escribe cada oración dos veces. La primera vez, cópiala. La segunda vez, haz que alguien lea la oración mientras la escribes.

1. I go to school.

2. My children go to school.

3. My children and I go to school.

1. _____ .

1. _____ .

2. _____ .

2. _____ .

3. _____ .

3. _____ .

✪ Lesson 7 Answers / Respuestas de la Lección 7

Multiple-choice questions / Preguntas de opción múltiple
1. b. two
2. b. four
3. a. vice president
4. d. cabinet
5. d. speaker of the House of Representatives
6. b. 35 years old
7. b. the vice president

Circle the correct answer / Encierra en un círculo la respuesta correcta.

1. What is one requirement to be president?
   born in Canada   (natural-born citizen of the United States)

2. Who becomes president if the president dies?
   first lady   (vice president)

3. What special group advises the President?
   Congress   (cabinet)

4. Who becomes president if the president and vice president die?
   (speaker of the House of Representatives)   Congress

5. How many terms can a president serve?
   (two)   three

"Yes" or "no" questions / Preguntas de "sí" o "no"

(Yes)　No　To become president, you must be a natural-born citizen of the United States.

(Yes)　No　The cabinet advises the president.

(Yes)　No　The duty of the executive branch is to enforce laws.

Yes　(No)　The first lady becomes president if the president dies.

(Yes)　No　The executive branch of the government includes the president, vice president, and cabinet.

(Yes)　No　The president can serve two terms in office.

Yes　(No)　To become president, you must be at least 50 years old.

Review Quiz 2 / Prueba de repaso 2

Mark the answers for each question on this sheet. The correct answers can be found on the last page of the quiz. / Marca las respuestas a las preguntas siguientes. Las respuestas correctas se encuentran en la última página de la prueba de repaso.

1. (a) (b) (c) (d)   8. (a) (b) (c) (d)

2. (a) (b) (c) (d)   9. (a) (b) (c) (d)

3. (a) (b) (c) (d)   10. (a) (b) (c) (d)

4. (a) (b) (c) (d)   11. (a) (b) (c) (d)

5. (a) (b) (c) (d)   12. (a) (b) (c) (d)

6. (a) (b) (c) (d)   13. (a) (b) (c) (d)

7. (a) (b) (c) (d)

1. How many times can a representative be re-elected?
   a. one
   b. two
   c. three
   d. no limit

2. For how long do we elect the representatives?
   a. two years
   b. three years
   c. four years
   d. five years

3. How many representatives are there in Congress?
   a. 435
   b. 100
   c. 2
   d. 500

4. What are the duties of the Supreme Court?
a. enforce the laws
b. make laws
c. interpret laws
d. declare war

5. Who is the chief justice of the Supreme Court?
a. John Roberts
b. George W. Bush
c. Al Gore
d. Condoleezza Rice

6. How many Supreme Court justices are there?
a. one
b. five
c. seven
d. nine

7. What is the highest court in the United States?
a. Supreme Court
b. federal court
c. city court
d. state court

8. For how long do we elect the president?
a. two years
b. six years
c. four years
d. three years

9. Who elects the president?
   a. Congress
   b. the Electoral College
   c. the Supreme Court
   d. the people

10. Who is the vice president today?
   a. Al Gore
   b. Richard Cheney
   c. Bill Clinton
   d. Henry Kissinger

11. Who is the president of the United States today?
   a. George W. Bush
   b. Bill Clinton
   c. Richard Cheney
   d. Al Gore

12. Who was the first president of the United States?
   a. Thomas Jefferson
   b. Benjamin Franklin
   c. George Washington
   d. Abraham Lincoln

13. What is the job of the executive branch?
   a. make laws
   b. interpret laws
   c. enforce laws
   d. vote

Review Quiz 2 Answers / Respuestas de la prueba de repaso 2

1. d. no limit
2. a. two years
3. a. 435
4. c. interpret laws
5. a. John Roberts
6. d. nine
7. a. Supreme Court
8. c. four years
9. b. the Electoral College
10. b. Richard Cheney
11. a. George W. Bush
12. c. George Washington
13. c. enforce laws

Lesson 8 / Lección 8

More about the President /
Más acerca del presidente

✪ Words to Know / Palabras claves

inaugurated: sworn into office (puesto en oficina a través de un juramento)

White House: home of the president (casa donde vive el presidente)

✪ About the President / Sobre el presidente

The president is the head executive of the United States. We vote for the president in November. Then, in January, the new president is **inaugurated**. During the president's term of office, the president lives in the **White House** in Washington, D.C.

El presidente es la cabeza ejecutiva de los Estados Unidos. Votamos por el presidente en noviembre. Luego en enero, el nuevo presidente asume su mandato. Durante el término como presidente, vive en la **Casa Blanca** en Washington, D.C.

President
- elected in November
- inaugurated in January
- lives in White House in Washington, D.C.

Presidente
- elegido en noviembre
- juramentado en enero
- vive en la Casa Blanca en Washington, D.C.

✪ Repetition / Repetición

Repeat these questions and answers out loud. / Repite estas preguntas y respuestas en voz alta.

1. What is the White House?
President's official home in Washington, D.C.

2. In what month do we vote for the president?
November

3. In what month is the new president inaugurated?
January

4. Who is the head executive of the United States?
the president

✪ Exercises / Ejercicios

Los ejercicios siguientes han sido diseñados para familiarizarte con el material de esta lección. El verdadero examen de ciudadanía puede ser oral o un examen de respuestas múltiples.

Multiple-choice questions / Preguntas de opción múltiple

The following exercises have been designed to familiarize you with the material of this lesson. The actual citizenship test may be oral or written. / Marca las respuestas a las preguntas siguientes. Las respuestas a estos ejercicios se encuentran en la última página de esta lección.

1. (a)   (b)   (c)   (d)   **3.** (a)   (b)   (c)   (d)

2. (a)   (b)   (c)   (d)   **4.** (a)   (b)   (c)   (d)

1. We vote for the president in which month?
   a. October
   b. November
   c. December
   d. January

2. The president is inaugurated in which month?
   a. October
   b. November
   c. December
   d. January

3. What is the president's official home called?
   a. the Capitol
   b. the White House
   c. the Supreme Court
   d. the Oval Office

4. Who is the head executive of the United States?
   a. the president
   b. the cabinet
   c. the chief justice
   d. the vice president

Matching questions / Preguntas para emparejar

Answer each question with the appropriate letter from the right column. / Relaciona cada pregunta con la letra más apropiada de la columna derecha.

____ the president's official home	A. January
____ we vote for the president during this month	B. White House
____ the president is inaugurated during this month	C. Washington, D.C.
____ the White House is located here	D. November

"Yes" or "no" questions / Preguntas de "sí" o "no"

Yes   No   The White House is located in Philadelphia, Pennsylvania.

Yes   No   The White House is the president's official home.

Yes   No   The president is inaugurated in November.

Yes   No   We vote for the president in January.

Yes   No   The cabinet is the president's official home.

Yes   No   The White House is located in Washington, D.C.

Yes   No   The president is inaugurated in January.

Yes   No   We vote for the president in November.

✪ Dictation Practice / Práctica de dictado

Write each sentence twice. The first time, copy it. The second time, don't look at it. Have someone read it aloud while you write it. / Escribe cada oración dos veces. La primera vez, cópiala. La segunda vez, haz que alguien lea la oración mientras la escribes.

1. My daughter is happy.

2. My family is happy to be in the United States.

3. We are happy to be here.

1. _____ .

1. _____ .

2. _____ .

2. _____ .

3. _____ .

3. _____ .

✪ Lesson 8 Answers / Respuestas de la Lección 8

Multiple-choice questions / Preguntas de opción múltiple

1. b. November
2. d. January
3. b. White House
4. a. the president

Matching questions / Preguntas para emparejar

_B_ the president's official home
_D_ we vote for the president during this month
_A_ the president is inaugurated during this month
_C_ the White House is located here

A. January
B. White House
C. Washington, D.C.
D. November

"Yes" or "no" questions / Preguntas de "sí" o "no"

Yes (No) The White House is located in Philadelphia, Pennsylvania.

(Yes) No The White House is the president's official home.

Yes (No) The president is inaugurated in November.

Yes (No) We vote for the president in January.

Yes (No) The cabinet is the president's official home.

(Yes) No The White House is located in Washington, D.C.

(Yes) No The president is inaugurated in January.

(Yes) No We vote for the president in November.

Lesson 9 / Lección 9

Head Executives / Jefes del ejecutivo

✪ Words to Know / Palabras claves

governor: leader of a state (gobernador)

head executive: the leader or person in charge (jefe del ejecutivo)

mayor: leader of a city (alcalde)

✪ About Head Executives / Sobre el jefe del ejecutivo

The **head executive** of the United States is the president. The president signs some bills into law and vetoes others. The president is also commander in chief of the U.S. military. George Washington was the first commander in chief of the U.S. military. The head executive of a state is the **governor**. The head executive of a city is a **mayor**.

El jefe de ejecutivo de los Estados Unidos es el presidente. El presidente firma las declaraciones y las convierte en ley y rechaza a otros. El presidente es también comandante en jefe de las fuerzas armadas de los Estados Unidos. George Washington fue el primer comandante en jefe de las fuerzas armadas estadounidenses. El jefe ejecutivo de un estado es el **gobernador** y el jefe ejecutivo de una ciudad es el **alcalde.**

Head Executive of the United States
- president
  - signs bills into law
  - vetoes bills
  - commander in chief of the U.S. military

Head Executive of a State
- governor

El jefe del ejecutivo de los Estados Unidos
- presidente
  - firma declaraciones y las convierte en ley
  - rechaza a declaraciones
  - comandante en jefe de las fuerzas armadas de los Estados Unidos

El jefe del ejecutivo en de un estado
- gobernador

Head Executive of City
- mayor

El jefe del ejecutivo de una ciudad
- alcalde

✪ Repetition / Repetición

Repeat these questions and answers out loud. / Repite estas preguntas y respuestas en voz alta.

1. What is the head executive of a state government called?
governor

2. What is the head executive of a city government called?
mayor

3. Who signs bills into law and vetoes bills?
the president

4. Who is commander in chief of the U.S. military?
the president

5. Who was the first commander in chief of the U.S. military?
George Washington

✪ Exercises / Ejercicios

Los ejercicios siguientes han sido diseñados para familiarizarte con el material de esta lección. El verdadero examen de ciudadanía puede ser oral o un examen de respuestas múltiples.

Multiple-choice questions / Preguntas de opción múltiple
The following exercises have been designed to familiarize you with the material of this lesson. The actual citizenship test may be oral or written. / Marca las respuestas a las preguntas siguientes. Las respuestas a estos ejercicios se encuentran en la última página de esta lección.

1. (a)   (b)   (c)   (d)   **3.** (a)   (b)   (c)   (d)

2. (a)   (b)   (c)   (d)   **4.** (a)   (b)   (c)   (d)

1. Who signs bills into law and vetoes bills?
   a. the president
   b. the vice president
   c. the speaker of the House
   d. Congress

2. Who was the first commander in chief of the U.S. military?
   a. Bill Clinton
   b. John Adams
   c. Abraham Lincoln
   d. George Washington

3. What is the head of a city government called?
   a. president
   b. governor
   c. mayor
   d. cabinet

4. What is the head of a state government called?
   a. president
   b. governor
   c. mayor
   d. cabinet

Circle the correct answer / Encierra en un círculo la respuesta correcta.

1. The _____ signs a bill into law.
Congress   president

2. The head executive of a city government is the _____.
governor   mayor

3. The _____ is commander in chief of the U.S. military.
president   citizen

4. The _____ is head executive of a state government.
president   governor

5. The first commander in chief of the U.S. military was _____.
George Washington   Abraham Lincoln

"Yes" or "no" questions / Preguntas de "sí" o "no"

Yes   No   The governor is the head executive of a city government.

Yes   No   The president signs a bill into law.

Yes   No   George Washington was the first commander in chief of the U.S. military.

Yes   No   The mayor is the head executive of a city government.

Yes   No   George W. Bush is the commander in chief of the U.S. military today.

Yes   No   The president is the head executive of the United States.

Yes   No   The mayor is the head executive of a state government.

Yes   No   The president has the power to veto bills.

✪ Dictation Practice / Práctica de dictado

Write each sentence twice. The first time, copy it. The second time, don't look at it. Have someone read it aloud while you write it. / Escribe cada oración dos veces. La primera vez, cópiala. La segunda vez, haz que alguien lea la oración mientras la escribes.

1. I believe in freedom.

2. I believe in the Constitution.

3. I believe in freedom and the Constitution.

1. _____.

1. _____.

2. _____.

2. _____.

3. _____.

3. _____.

✪ Lesson 9 Answers / Respuestas de la Lección 9

Multiple-choice questions / Preguntas de opción múltiple
1. a. the president
2. d. George Washington
3. c. mayor
4. b. governor

Circle the correct answer / Encierra en un círculo la respuesta correcta.

1. The _____ signs a bill into law.
   Congress   (president)

2. The head executive of a city government is the _____.
   governor   (mayor)

3. The _____ is commander in chief of the U.S. military.
   (president)   citizen

4. The _____ is head executive of a state government.
   president   (governor)

5. The first commander in chief of the U.S. military was _____.
   (George Washington)   Abraham Lincoln

"Yes" or "no" questions / Preguntas de "sí" o "no"

Yes   (No)   The governor is the head executive of a city government.

(Yes)   No   The president signs a bill into law.

(Yes)   No   George Washington was the first commander in chief of the U.S. military.

(Yes)   No   The mayor is the head executive of a city government.

(Yes)   No   George W. Bush is the commander in chief of the U.S. military today.

(Yes)   No   The president is the head executive of the United States.

Yes   (No)   The mayor is the head executive of a state government.

(Yes)   No   The president has the power to veto bills.

Review Quiz 3 / Prueba de repaso 3

Mark the answers for each question on this sheet. The correct answers can be found on the last page of the quiz. / Marca las respuestas a las siguientes preguntas. Las respuestas correctas se encuentran en la última página de la prueba de repaso.

1. (a) (b) (c) (d)   9. (a) (b) (c) (d)

2. (a) (b) (c) (d)   10. (a) (b) (c) (d)

3. (a) (b) (c) (d)   11. (a) (b) (c) (d)

4. (a) (b) (c) (d)   12. (a) (b) (c) (d)

5. (a) (b) (c) (d)   13. (a) (b) (c) (d)

6. (a) (b) (c) (d)

7. (a) (b) (c) (d)

8. (a) (b) (c) (d)

1. Who becomes president if the president and vice president die?
   a. Congress
   b. chief justice of the Supreme Court
   c. speaker of the House of Representatives
   d. governor

2. How many terms can a president serve?
   a. two
   b. three
   c. one
   d. no limit

3. Who becomes president of the United States if the president dies?
   a. vice president
   b. speaker of the House of Representatives
   c. mayor
   d. senator

4. What is one requirement to be president?
   a. natural-born citizen of the United States
   b. lived in Canada
   c. be male
   d. speak Spanish

5. What is the cabinet's job?
   a. to declare war
   b. to interpret laws
   c. to command the military
   d. to advise the president

6. Who was the first commander in chief of the U.S. military?
   a. Thomas Jefferson
   b. Bill Clinton
   c. George Bush
   d. George Washington

7. Who is commander in chief of the U.S. military?
   a. Bill Clinton
   b. George W. Bush
   c. George Washington
   d. Abraham Lincoln

8. Who signs bills into law?
   a. Congress
   b. the Supreme Court
   c. the vice president
   d. the president

9. What is the head executive of a city government called?
   a. mayor
   b. governor
   c. president
   d. senator

10. What is the head executive of a state government called?
   a. president
   b. mayor
   c. governor
   d. Supreme Court justice

11. What is the White House?
   a. where Congress meets
   b. the president's official home
   c. the governor's home
   d. where the Supreme Court meets

12. In what month do we vote for president?
   a. October
   b. January
   c. December
   d. November

13. In what month is the president inaugurated?
   a. March
   b. April
   c. September
   d. January

Review Quiz 3 Answers /
Respuestas de la prueba de repaso 3

1. c. the speaker of the House of Representatives
2. a. two
3. a. vice president
4. a. natural-born citizen of the United States
5. d. to advise the president
6. d. George Washington
7. b. George W. Bush
8. d. the president
9. a. mayor
10. c. governor
11. b. the president's official home
12. d. November
13. d. January

Lesson 10 / Lección 10

The Constitution / La Constitución

✪ Words to Know / Palabras claves

amendments: changes or additions to the Constitution (enmiendas)

Constitution: the supreme law of the United States (la ley suprema de los Estados Unidos)

Rule of Law: The idea that everyone must follow the law and no one is above the law (la idea que nadie está sobre la ley y todos tienen que obedecerla)

✪ About the Constitution / Sobre la Constitución

The supreme law of the land is the **Constitution**. The basis of the Constitution is the idea of **rule of law**, which means that no one is above the law. The Constitution sets up the government and lists the basic rights of all Americans. It also divides power between the federal government in Washington, D.C. and the state governments. It begins with the words, "We the people of the United States." It was written in 1787. It can be changed. Changes to the **Constitution** are called **amendments**. There have been 27 **amendments** to the **Constitution**.

La ley suprema de los Estados Unidos es la **Constitución**. La base de la Constitución es la idea de la regla de la ley, que significa que nadie está sobre la ley. La Constitución establece el gobierno y enumera los derechos básicos de todos estadounidenses. También divide el poder entre el **gobierno federal** Washington, D.C. y los gobiernos de los estados. Ésta comienza con la frase, "Nosotros, la gente de los Estados Unidos." La Constitución fue escrita en 1787 y tiene la virtud de poder ser modificada. Estas modificaciones se llaman enmiendas. La Constitutión tiene 27 enmiendas.

Constitution
- written in 1787
- begins with "We the people of the United States"

Constitución
- escrita en 1787
- empieza con "Nosotros, la gente de los Estados Unidos"

- is the supreme law of the United States
- sets up the government
- lists rights of Americans
- can be changed
- changes are called amendments
- has 27 amendments

- es la ley suprema de los Estados Unidos
- establece el gobierno
- enumera los derechos de estadounidenses
- puede ser cambiada
- los cambios se llaman enmiendas
- tiene 27 enmiendas

✪ Repetition / Repetición

Repeat these questions and answers out loud. / Repite estas preguntas y respuestas en voz alta.

1. What is the Constitution?
the supreme law of the land

2. Can the Constitution be changed?
yes

3. What do we call changes to the Constitution?
amendments

4. How many amendments are there?
27 (twenty-seven)

5. What is the supreme law of the United States?
Constitution

6. When was the Constitution written?
1787

7. What are the opening words of the Constitution?
"We the People of the United States"

8. What is one power the Constitution gives to the federal government?
many answers, including the right to declare war and to collect income tax

✪ Exercises / Ejercicios

Los ejercicios siguientes han sido diseñados para familiarizarte con el material de esta lección. El verdadero examen de ciudadanía puede ser oral o un examen de respuestas múltiples.

Multiple-choice questions / Preguntas de opción múltiple

The following exercises have been designed to familiarize you with the material of this lesson. The actual citizenship test may be oral or written. / Marca las respuestas a las preguntas siguientes. Las respuestas a estos ejercicios se encuentran en la última página de esta lección.

1. (a)   (b)   (c)   (d)   4. (a)   (b)   (c)   (d)

2. (a)   (b)   (c)   (d)   5. (a)   (b)   (c)   (d)

3. (a)   (b)   (c)   (d)

1. What is the supreme law of the land?
   a. the president
   b. the cabinet
   c. the Constitution
   d. the Capitol

2. What is a change to the Constitution called?
   a. assurance
   b. amendment
   c. addition
   d. deletion

3. When was the Constitution written?
   a. 1945
   b. 1787
   c. 1776
   d. 1800

4. What is the Constitution?
   a. the supreme law of the land
   b. an award-winning book
   c. the Supreme Court
   d. an amendment

5. How many amendments to the Constitution are there?
   a. 24
   b. 25
   c. 26
   d. 27

Circle the correct answer / Encierra en un círculo la respuesta correcta.

1. There are _____ amendments to the Constitution.
   24   27

2. A change to the Constitution is an _____.
   amendment   appeal

3. The Constitution is the supreme _____ of the land.
   law   crime

4. The Constitution _____ be changed.
   can   cannot

5. The supreme law of the land is the _____.
   Constitution   Congress

6. The Constitution was written in _____.
   1787   1776

"Yes" or "no" questions / Preguntas de "sí" o "no"

Yes   No   The Constitution is the supreme law of the land.

Yes   No   A change to the Constitution is called an amendment.

Yes   No   The Constitution cannot be changed.

Yes   No   The Constitution was written in 1776.

Yes   No   There are 27 amendments to the Constitution.

Yes   No   The Constitution was written in 1787.

Yes   No   There are 24 amendments to the Constitution.

✪ Dictation Practice / Práctica de dictado

Write each sentence twice. The first time, copy it. The second time, don't look at it. Have someone read it aloud while you write it. / Escribe cada oración dos veces. La primera vez, cópiala. La segunda vez, haz que alguien lea la oración mientras la escribes.

1. The sky is blue.

2. My dog is brown.

3. I like my brown dog and the blue sky.

1. _____ .

1. _____ .

2. _____ .

2. _____ .

3. _____ .

3. _____ .

✪ Lesson 10 Answers / Respuestas de la Lección 10

Multiple-choice questions / Preguntas de opción múltiple
1. c. the Constitution
2. b. amendment
3. b. 1787
4. a. the supreme law of the land
5. d. 27

Circle the correct answer / Encierra en un círculo la respuesta correcta.

1. There are _____ amendments to the Constitution.
   24   (27)

2. A change to the Constitution is an _____.
   (amendment)   appeal

3. The Constitution is the supreme _____ of the land.
   (law)   crime

4. The Constitution _____ be changed.
   (can)   cannot

5. The supreme law of the land is the _____.
   (Constitution)   Congress

6. The Constitution was written in _____.
   (1787)   1776

"Yes" or "no" questions / Preguntas de "sí" o "no"

(Yes)   No   The Constitution is the supreme law of the land.

(Yes)   No   A change to the Constitution is called an amendment.

Yes   (No)   The Constitution cannot be changed.

Yes   (No)   The Constitution was written in 1776.

(Yes)   No   There are 27 amendments to the Constitution.

(Yes)   No   The Constitution was written in 1787.

Yes   (No)   There are 24 amendments to the Constitution.

Lesson 11 / Lección 11

More about the Constitution / Más sobre de la Constitución

✪ Words to Know / Palabras claves

Bill of Rights	the first ten amendment to the Constitution (Declaración de Derechos)
introduction:	the first part (introducción)
preamble:	the introduction to the Constitution (preámbulo)
supreme law:	the highest, most important law (la ley más alta y más importante)
Federalist Papers:	documents that supported the passage of the Constitution (documentos que apoyaron al pasaje de la Constitución)
Constitutional Convention:	convention in 1787 where the Constitution was written (la convención en 1787 donde la Constitución fue escrita)
Benjamin Franklin:	oldest member of the Constitutional Convention (el miembro más viejo de la Convención Constitucional)

✪ More about the Constitution / Más sobre de la Constitución

The Constitution is the **supreme law** of the land. The **introduction** to the Constitution is called the **Preamble**. The first ten amendments to the Constitution are called the **Bill of Rights**. The first amendment in the **Bill of Rights** grants freedom of speech. Everyone in the United States is protected by the Constitution and the Bill of Rights, including non-citizens. The Constitution was written at the **Constitutional Convention** in 1787. **Benjamin Franklin** was the oldest member of this convention. Before the Constitution there were a series of documents called the **Federalist Papers**, written by **Alexander Hamilton**, **John Jay**, and **James Madison**, which supported the passage of the Constitution.

La Constitución es la **ley suprema** del país. La **introducción** a la Constitución se conoce como el **Preámbulo.** Las diez primeras enmiendas a la Constitución se llaman la **Declaración de Derechos.** La primera enmienda permite la libertad de expresión. Todos los habitantes de los Estados Unidos, incluso los no-ciudadanos, son protegidos por la Constitución y la **Declaración de Derechos.** La Constitución fue escrito en la **Convención Constitucional** en 1787. **Benjamín Franklin** era el miembro más viejo de la convención. Antes de la Constitución había una serie de documentos llamados los **Papeles Federalistas,** escritos por **Alexander Hamilton, John Jay,** y **James Madison,** y apoyaron el pasaje de la Constitución.

Constitution
- has **introduction** called **preamble**
- is **supreme law** of the land
- protects everyone in the United States, including non-citizens

Constitución
- Tiene una **introducción** llamada el **preámbulo**
- Es la **ley suprema** del país
- protege a todos los habitantes de los Estados Unidos, incluso no-ciudadanos

Bill of Rights
- the first ten amendments to the Constitution
- grants freedom of speech
- protects everyone in the United States, including non-citizens

Declaración de los Derechos
- las diez primeras enmiendas a la Constitución
- ofrece la libertad de expresión
- protege a todos los habitantes de los Estados Unidos, incluso a los no-ciudadanos

✪ Repetition / Repetición

Repeat these questions and answers out loud. / Repite estas preguntas y respuestas en voz alta.

1. What is the Bill of Rights?
the first ten amendments to the Constitution

2. Where does the freedom of speech come from?
the First Amendment

3. What are the first ten amendments called?
the Bill of Rights

4. Whose rights are guaranteed by the Constitution and the Bill of Rights?
everyone in the United States, including non-citizens

5. What is the introduction to the Constitution called?
the preamble

6. What document written by Alexander Hamilton, James Madison, and John Jay came before the Constitution?
the Federalist Papers

7. Who was the oldest member of the Constitutional Convention?
Benjamin Franklin

✪ Exercises / Ejercicios

Los ejercicios siguientes han sido diseñados para familiarizarte con el material de esta lección. El verdadero examen de ciudadanía puede ser oral o un examen de respuestas múltiples.

Multiple-choice questions / Preguntas de opción múltiple
The following exercises have been designed to familiarize you with the material of this lesson. The actual citizenship test may be oral or written. / Marca las respuestas a las preguntas siguientes. Las respuestas a estos ejercicios se encuentran en la última página de esta lección.

1. (a) (b) (c) (d)   **4.** (a) (b) (c) (d)

2. (a) (b) (c) (d)   **5.** (a) (b) (c) (d)

3. (a) (b) (c) (d)   **6.** (a) (b) (c) (d)

1. What are the first ten amendments to the Constitution called?
   a. the preamble
   b. the introduction
   c. the Bill of Rights
   d. the Book of Law

2. What is the Bill of Rights?
   a. the last ten amendments to the Constitution
   b. changes to the Declaration of Statehood
   c. additions to the president's speech
   d. the first ten amendments to the Constitution

3. Where does freedom of speech come from?
   a. the Bill of Rights
   b. the president
   c. the Pilgrims
   d. the Supreme Court

4. Whose rights are guaranteed by the Constitution?
   a. Canadians
   b. Europeans
   c. American citizens only
   d. everyone in the United States, including non-citizens

5. What is the introduction to the Constitution called?
   a. the preamble
   b. the epilogue
   c. the Bill of Rights
   d. the Declaration of Independence

6. Who was the oldest representative at the Constitutional Convention?
   a. Benjamin Franklin
   b. George Washington
   c. Thomas Jefferson
   d. Patrick Henry

Circle the correct answer / Encierra en un círculo la respuesta correcta.

1. the first ten amendments
   Bill of Rights   Congress

2. the introduction to the Constitution
   preamble   Bill of Rights

3. freedom of speech comes from here
   president   Bill of Rights

4. the Bill of Rights
   first ten amendments   Supreme Court

"Yes" or "no" questions / Preguntas de "sí" o "no"

Yes   No   The Constitution is the supreme law of the land.

Yes   No   The first ten amendments to the Constitution are called the Bill of Rights.

Yes   No   Freedom of speech comes from the Bill of Rights.

Yes   No   The Bill of Rights is the first 12 amendments to the Constitution.

Yes   No   The introduction to the Constitution is called the preamble.

Yes   No   Everyone in the United States is protected by the Bill of Rights, including non-citizens.

Yes   No   Thomas Jefferson wrote the Federalist Papers

Yes   No   The Bill of Rights is the first ten amendments to the Constitution.

Yes   No   The conclusion to the Constitution is called the preamble.

✪ Dictation Practice / Práctica de dictado

Write each sentence twice. The first time, copy it. The second time, don't look at it. Have someone read it aloud while you write it. / Escribe cada oración dos veces. La primera vez, cópiala. La segunda vez, haz que alguien lea la oración mientras la escribes.

1. There is a bird.

2. The bird is in the tree.

3. There is a bird in the tree.

1. _____.

1. _____.

2. _____.

2. _____.

3. _____.

3. _____.

✪ Lesson 11 Answers / Respuestas de la Lección 11

Multiple-choice questions / Preguntas de opción múltiple
1. c. the Bill of Rights
2. d. the first ten amendments to the Constitution
3. a. the Bill of Rights
4. d. everyone in the United States, including non-citizens
5. a. the preamble
6. a. Benjamin Franklin

Circle the correct answer / Encierra en un círculo la respuesta correcta.

1. the first ten amendments
(Bill of Rights)   Congress

2. the introduction to the Constitution
(preamble)   Bill of Rights

3. freedom of speech comes from here
President   (Bill of Rights)

4. the Bill of Rights
(first ten amendments)   Supreme Court

"Yes" or "no" questions / Preguntas de "sí" o "no"

(Yes)   No   The Constitution is the supreme law of the land.

(Yes)   No   The first ten amendments to the Constitution are called the Bill of Rights.

(Yes)   No   Freedom of speech comes from the Bill of Rights.

Yes   (No)   The Bill of Rights is the first 12 amendments to the Constitution.

(Yes)   No   The introduction to the Constitution is called the preamble.

(Yes)   No   Everyone in the United States is protected by the Bill of Rights, including non-citizens.

Yes   (No)   Thomas Jefferson wrote the Federalist Papers

(Yes)   No   The Bill of Rights is the first ten amendments to the Constitution.

Yes   (No)   The conclusion to the Constitution is called the preamble.

Lesson 12 / Lección 12

The Bill of Rights / La Declaración de Derechos

✪ Words to Know / Palabras claves

bear arms: carry a gun (llevar armas)

freedom of religion: the right to practice any religion, or no religion (el derecho de practicar cualquier religión, o ninguna religión)

✪ About the Bill of Rights / Sobre la Declaración de Derechos

As you know, the Constitution is the supreme law of the land, and the first ten amendments to the Constitution are called the **Bill of Rights**. Everyone in the United States is protected by the **Bill of Rights**, including non-citizens. The **Bill of Rights** includes the following points:

- Everyone has the freedom of speech, press, and religion.
- Everyone has the right to **bear arms**.
- Government may not put soldiers in people's homes.
- A person may not be **tried** for the same crime twice.

Como ya sabes, a Constitución es la ley suprema del país y las diez primeras enmiendas a la Constitución se llaman la **Declaración de Derechos**. Todos en los Estados Unidos son protegidos por la **Declaración de Derechos**, incluso los no-ciudadanos. Algunos puntos de la **Declaración de Derechos** son

- Todos tienen la libertad de expresión, prensa y religión.
- Todos tienen la libertad de **llevar armas**.
- El gobierno no puede poner a soldados en las casas de la gente.
- Nadie puede ser **juzgado** dos veces por el mismo crimen.

- A person charged with a crime has rights to a trial and a lawyer.
- People are protected from unreasonable fines or cruel punishment.

- Una persona acusada de un crimen tiene derecho a un abogado y a un juicio.
- La gente es protegida contra multas excesivas o castigos crueles.

✪ Repetition / Repetición

Repeat these questions and answers out loud. / Repite estas preguntas y respuestas en voz alta.

1. What are the first ten amendments called?
The Bill of Rights

2. What are the freedoms guaranteed by the Bill of Rights?
- *Everyone has the freedom of speech, press, and religion.*
- *Everyone has the right to bear arms.*
- *Government may not put soldiers in people's homes.*
- *Government may not search or take a person's property without a warrant.*
- *A person may not be tried for the same crime twice.*
- *A person charged with a crime has rights including the right to a trial and a lawyer.*
- *People are protected from unreasonable fines or cruel punishment.*

3. Name one right guaranteed by the First Amendment.
freedom of speech, press, religion, peaceable assembly, and change of government

4. The First Amendment provides freedom of religion. What does freedom of religion mean?
the right to practice any religion, or no religion at all

✪ Exercises / Ejercicios

Los ejercicios siguientes han sido diseñados para familiarizarte con el material de esta lección. El verdadero examen de ciudadanía puede ser oral o un examen de respuestas múltiples.

Multiple-choice questions / Preguntas de opción múltiple

The following exercises have been designed to familiarize you with the material of this lesson. The actual citizenship test may be oral or written. / Marca las respuestas a las preguntas siguientes. Las respuestas a estos ejercicios se encuentran en la última página de esta lección.

1. ⓐ ⓑ ⓒ ⓓ   **3.** ⓐ ⓑ ⓒ ⓓ

2. ⓐ ⓑ ⓒ ⓓ   **4.** ⓐ ⓑ ⓒ ⓓ

1. How many amendments make up the Bill of Rights?
   a. three
   b. ten
   c. fifty
   d. thirteen

2. Which freedom is guaranteed by the Bill of Rights?
   a. right to pay taxes
   b. right to free speech
   c. right to get paid for your work
   d. right to govern your neighbor

3. Which freedom is guaranteed by the Bill of Rights?
   a. A person may not be tried for the same crime twice.
   b. A person may walk on the moon.
   c. A person may kill his or her neighbor.
   d. A person charged with a crime may not get a trial.

4. Which freedom is guaranteed by the Bill of Rights?
   a. freedom to steal from your neighbor
   b. freedom of speech
   c. freedom to fight the government
   d. freedom to set off a bomb

"Yes" or "no" questions / Preguntas de "sí" o "no"

Yes   No   The Constitution is the supreme law of the land.

Yes   No   The first ten amendments to the Constitution are called the Bill of Rights.

Yes   No   Freedom of speech comes from the Bill of Rights.

Yes   No   The right to bear arms comes from the Bill of Rights.

Yes   No   Everyone is protected by the Bill of Rights, including non-citizens.

Yes   No   The Bill of Rights is the first ten amendments to the Constitution.

Yes   No   A person in the United States may not be tried for the same crime twice.

Yes   No   People in the United States are not protected from unreasonable fines.

Yes   No   Freedom of religion comes from the Bill of Rights.

Yes   No   The government may put soldiers in people's homes.

Yes   No   Everyone in the United States must practice a religion.

✪ Dictation Practice / Práctica de dictado

Write each sentence twice. The first time, copy it. The second time, don't look at it. Have someone read it aloud while you write it. / Escribe cada oración dos veces. La primera vez, cópiala. La segunda vez, haz que alguien lea la oración mientras la escribes.

1. I have four children.

2. I live with my children.

3. I live with my four children.

1. _____ .

1. _____ .

2. _____ .

2. _____ .

3. _____ .

3. _____ .

✪ Lesson 12 Answers / Respuestas de la Lección 12

Multiple-choice questions / Preguntas de opción múltiple
1. b. ten
2. b. right to free speech
3. a. a person may not be tried for the same crime twice
4. b. freedom of speech

"Yes" or "no" questions / Preguntas de "sí" o "no"

(Yes) No   The Constitution is the supreme law of the land.

(Yes) No   The first ten amendments to the Constitution are called the Bill of Rights.

(Yes) No   Freedom of speech comes from the Bill of Rights.

(Yes) No   The right to bear arms comes from the Bill of Rights.

(Yes) No   Everyone is protected by the Bill of Rights, including non-citizens.

(Yes) No   The Bill of Rights is the first ten amendments to the Constitution.

(Yes) No   A person in the United States may not be tried for the same crime twice.

Yes (No)   People in the United States are not protected from unreasonable fines.

(Yes) No   Freedom of religion comes from the Bill of Rights.

Yes (No)   The government may put soldiers in people's homes.

Yes (No)   Everyone in the United States must practice a religion.

Review Quiz 4 / Prueba de repaso 4

Mark the answers for each question on this sheet. The correct answers can be found on the last page of the quiz. / Marca las respuestas a las preguntas siguientes. Las respuestas correctas se encuentran en la última página de la prueba de repaso.

1. ⓐ ⓑ ⓒ ⓓ   7. ⓐ ⓑ ⓒ ⓓ

2. ⓐ ⓑ ⓒ ⓓ   8. ⓐ ⓑ ⓒ ⓓ

3. ⓐ ⓑ ⓒ ⓓ   9. ⓐ ⓑ ⓒ ⓓ

4. ⓐ ⓑ ⓒ ⓓ   10. ⓐ ⓑ ⓒ ⓓ

5. ⓐ ⓑ ⓒ ⓓ   11. ⓐ ⓑ ⓒ ⓓ

6. ⓐ ⓑ ⓒ ⓓ

1. When was the Constitution written?
   a. 1787
   b. 1789
   c. 1777
   d. 1749

2. What is the supreme law of the United States?
   a. the Declaration of Independence
   b. the Constitution
   c. the Supreme Court
   d. Congress

3. How many amendments are there?
   a. 23
   b. 25
   c. 26
   d. 27

4. What do we call a change to the Constitution?
   a. amendment
   b. objection
   c. law
   d. president

5. What is the Constitution?
   a. the supreme law of the land
   b. the Bill of Rights
   c. the House of Representatives
   d. the Declaration of Independence

6. What are the first ten amendments called?
   a. the Preamble
   b. the Constitution
   c. the Bill of Rights
   d. the Declaration of Independence

7. Whose rights are guaranteed by the Constitution?
   a. only citizens
   b. only the president
   c. only Congress
   d. both citizens and non-citizens

8. What is the introduction to the Constitution called?
   a. the Bill of Rights
   b. the supreme law of the land
   c. the preface
   d. the preamble

9. Where does the freedom of speech come from?
   a. the president
   b. Congress
   c. the Bill of Rights
   d. the Supreme Court

10. How does the preamble begin?
   a. "We the citizens"
   b. "We Americans"
   c. "We the People of the United States"
   d. "We the United States"

11. What is one right guaranteed by the Bill of Rights?
   a. freedom of speech
   b. freedom of marriage
   c. freedom to kill your neighbor
   d. freedom to rob your neighbor

Review Quiz 4 Answers / Respuestas de la prueba de repaso 4

1. a. 1787
2. b. the Constitution
3. d. 27
4. a. amendment
5. a. the supreme law of the land
6. c. the Bill of Rights
7. d. both citizens and non-citizens
8. d. the preamble
9. c. the Bill of Rights
10. c. "We the People of the United States"
11. a. freedom of speech

Lesson 13 / Lección 13

The Pilgrims / Los Peregrinos

✪ Words to Know / Palabras claves

Native Americans:	people living in America when the Pilgrims arrived (americanos indígenos)
Pilgrims:	people who came from England (Peregrinos)
Thanksgiving:	a holiday that was first celebrated by the pilgrims and the Native Americans (Día de acción de gracias)

✪ About the Pilgrims / Sobre los Peregrinos

The **Pilgrims** came to America from England for religious freedom. When they came to America, they met the **Native Americans**. The **Native Americans** helped the **Pilgrims**. In America, the first holiday the **Pilgrims** celebrated was **Thanksgiving**. They celebrated it with the **Native Americans**. Some examples of **Native American** tribes are the Cherokee, Navajo, Sioux, Apache, and Creek, but there are many more as well.

Los **Peregrinos** vinieron a América buscando libertad religiosa. Cuando llegaron a América, se encontraron con los americanos indígenos. **Los americanos indígenos** ayudaron a los Peregrinos. En América, el primer día feriado que **los Peregrinos** celebraron fue el día de acción de gracias. Ellos lo celebraron con **los americanos indígenos**. Algunos ejemplos de tribus **indígenas** son los Cherokee, los Navajo, los Sioux, los Apache y los Creek, pero existen muchas otras tambien.

Pilgrims
- were first colonists
- came from England
- came for religious freedom

Peregrinos
- fueron los primeros colonizadores
- vinieron por libertad religiosa

- met and got help from Native Americans
- celebrated the first Thanksgiving

- conocieron y recibieron ayuda de los americanos indígenos
- celebraron el primer día feriado, el Día de acción de gracias

✪ Repetition / Repetición

Repeat these questions and answers out loud. / Repite estas preguntas y respuestas en voz alta.

1. Why did the Pilgrims come to America?
   religious freedom

2. Who helped the Pilgrims in America?
   Native Americans

3. What holiday was celebrated for the first time by the American colonists?
   Thanksgiving

4. Who were the first American colonists?
   the Pilgrims

✪ Exercises / Ejercicios

Los ejercicios siguientes han sido diseñados para familiarizarte con el material de esta lección. El verdadero examen de ciudadanía puede ser oral o un examen de respuestas múltiples.

Multiple-choice questions / Preguntas de opción múltiple

The following exercises have been designed to familiarize you with the material of this lesson. The actual citizenship test may be oral or written. / Marca las respuestas a las preguntas siguientes. Las respuestas a estos ejercicios se encuentran en la última página de esta lección.

1. (a) (b) (c) (d)   4. (a) (b) (c) (d)

2. (a) (b) (c) (d)   5. (a) (b) (c) (d)

3. (a) (b) (c) (d)

1. Who did the Pilgrims meet when they came to America?
   a. Native Americans
   b. Europeans
   c. Canadians
   d. senators

2. Why did the Pilgrims come to America?
   a. to get rich
   b. for new homes
   c. religious freedom
   d. to leave their relatives

3. What holiday did the Pilgrims celebrate with the Native Americans?
   a. Thanksgiving
   b. Halloween
   c. Easter
   d. Valentine's Day

4. Who helped the Pilgrims when they arrived in America?
   a. animals
   b. Native Americans
   c. Mexicans
   d. Chinese

5. Where did the Pilgrims come from?
   a. France
   b. Mexico
   c. Russia
   d. England

Matching questions / Preguntas para emparejar

Answer each question with the appropriate letter from the right column. / Relaciona cada pregunta con la letra más apropiada de la columna derecha.

_____ helped the Pilgrims in America	A. Thanksgiving
_____ holiday celebrated by the American colonists	B. religious freedom
_____ reason pilgrims came to America	C. Native Americans

"Yes" or "no" questions / Preguntas de "sí" o "no"

Yes   No   The Native Americans helped the Pilgrims.

Yes   No   The Pilgrims came to America because they wanted a vacation.

Yes   No   Thanksgiving was the first holiday celebrated by the Pilgrims.

Yes   No   The Pilgrims came to America for religious freedom.

Yes   No   Easter was the first holiday celebrated by the Pilgrims.

✪ Dictation Practice / Práctica de dictado

Write each sentence twice. The first time, copy it. The second time, don't look at it. Have someone read it aloud while you write it. / Escribe cada oración dos veces. La primera vez, cópiala. La segunda vez, haz que alguien lea la oración mientras la escribes.

1. I drive a car.

2. My car is big and red.

3. I drive a big red car.

1. _____ .

1. _____ .

2. _____ .

2. _____ .

3. _____ .

3. _____ .

Multiple-choice questions / Preguntas de opción múltiple

1. a. Native Americans
2. c. religious freedom
3. a. Thanksgiving
4. b. Native Americans
5. d. England

Matching Answers

_C_ helped the pilgrims in America
_A_ holiday celebrated by the Pilgrims in America
_B_ reason pilgrims came to America

A. Thanksgiving
B. religious freedom
C. Native Americans

"Yes" or "no" questions / Preguntas de "sí" o "no"

(Yes)   No   The Native Americans helped the Pilgrims.

Yes   (No)   The Pilgrims came to America because they wanted a vacation.

(Yes)   No   Thanksgiving was the first holiday celebrated by the Pilgrims.

(Yes)   No   The Pilgrims came to America for religious freedom.

Yes   (No)   Easter was the first holiday celebrated by the Pilgrims.

Lesson 14 / Lección 14

The Colonies / Las colonias

✪ Words to Know / Palabras claves

colonies:	original 13 states in United States (13 estados originales de los Estados Unidos)
King George:	King of England who ruled over the colonies (rey de Inglaterra que gobernaba las colonias)

✪ About the Colonies / Sobre las colonias

The 13 original states were called the **colonies** before they became states. The original 13 **colonies** were Delaware, Pennsylvania, New Jersey, Georgia, Connecticut, Massachusetts, Maryland, South Carolina, New Hampshire, Virginia, New York, North Carolina, and Rhode Island. The **colonies** were ruled by the king of England, **King George**.

Originalmente, los 13 primeros territorios se llamaban **colonias.** Las 13 primeras **colonias** eran Delaware, Pennsylvania, New Jersey, Georgia, Connecticut, Massachusetts, Maryland, South Carolina, New Hampshire, Virginia, New York, North Carolina, and Rhode Island. Las **colonias** eran gobernadas por el rey de Inglaterra, el **Rey Jorge.**

Colonies (ruled by King George)

Connecticut	New York
Delaware	North Carolina
Georgia	Pennsylvania
Maryland	Rhode Island
Massachusetts	South Carolina
New Hampshire	Virginia
New Jersey	

Colonias (gobernadas por el rey Jorge)

Connecticut	New York
Delaware	North Carolina
Georgia	Pennsylvania
Maryland	Rhode Island
Massachusetts	South Carolina
New Hampshire	Virginia
New Jersey	

✪ Repetition / Repetición

Repeat these questions and answers out loud. / Repite estas preguntas y respuestas en voz alta.

1. What are the 13 original states called?
colonies

2. Can you name the original 13 states?
- *Connecticut*
- *Delaware*
- *Georgia*
- *Maryland*
- *Massachusetts*
- *New Hampshire*
- *New Jersey*
- *New York*
- *North Carolina*
- *Pennsylvania*
- *Rhode Island*
- *South Carolina*
- *Virginia*

✪ Exercises / Ejercicios

Los ejercicios siguientes han sido diseñados para familiarizarte con el material de esta lección. El verdadero examen de ciudadanía puede ser oral o un examen de respuestas múltiples.

Multiple-choice questions / Preguntas de opción múltiple

The following exercises have been designed to familiarize you with the material of this lesson. The actual citizenship test may be oral or written. / Marca las respuestas a las preguntas siguientes. Las respuestas a estos ejercicios se encuentran en la última página de esta lección.

1. (a) (b) (c) (d)   **3.** (a) (b) (c) (d)

2. (a) (b) (c) (d)

1. What were the 13 original states called?
   a. Native American cities
   b. colonies
   c. states
   d. settlements

2. Which state was a part of the 13 colonies?
   a. Connecticut
   b. California
   c. Washington
   d. Nevada

3. Which state was not a part of the 13 colonies?
   a. Illinios
   b. South Carolina
   c. Massachusetts
   d. New Jersey

Circle the correct answer / Encierra en un círculo la respuesta correcta.

1. The original 13 states were called the _____.
colonies   provinces

2. Name two of the original 13 states: _____ and _____.
Connecticut/New Hampshire   Texas/Maine

"Yes" or "no" questions / Preguntas de "sí" o "no"

Yes   No   The 13 original states were called the colonies.

Yes   No   New York was one of the colonies.

Yes   No   Texas was one of the colonies.

Yes   No   California was one of the original 13 states.

Yes   No   Georgia was one of the colonies.

✪ Dictation Practice / Práctica de dictado

Write each sentence twice. The first time, copy it. The second time, don't look at it. Have someone read it aloud while you write it. / Escribe cada oración dos veces. La primera vez, cópiala. La segunda vez, haz que alguien lea la oración mientras la escribes.

1. I live in a house.

2. I live in a blue house.

3. My house is nice.

1. _____ .

1. _____ .

2. _____ .

2. _____ .

3. _____ .

3. _____ .

✪ Lesson 14 Answers / Respuestas de la Lección 14

Multiple-choice questions / Preguntas de opción múltiple
1. b. colonies
2. a. Connecticut
3. a. Illinois

Circle the correct answer / Encierra en un círculo la respuesta correcta.

1. The original 13 states were called the _____.
   (colonies)   provinces

2. Name two of the original 13 states: _____ and _____.
   (Connecticut/New Hampshire)   Texas/Maine

"Yes" or "no" questions / Preguntas de "sí" o "no"

(Yes)   No   The 13 original states were called the colonies.

(Yes)   No   New York was one of the colonies.

Yes   (No)   Texas was one of the colonies.

Yes   (No)   California was one of the original 13 states.

(Yes)   No   Georgia was one of the colonies.

Lesson 15 / Lección 15

Declaration of Independence / La Declaración de Independencia

✪ Words to Know / Palabras claves

Declaration of Independence: written statement saying the colonies wanted to be free from England (declaración escrita que estableció que las colonias querían ser independientes de Inglaterra)

Independence Day: July 4th (el 4 de julio, el Día de independencía)

✪ About the Declaration of Independence / Sobre la Declaración de Independencia

The colonies were not happy being ruled by England and wanted to be independent. Thomas Jefferson wrote the **Declaration of Independence**. The Declaration said that the colonies wanted to be free from England. The basic belief of the **Declaration of Independence** is that all men are created equal. It states that everyone has the right to life, liberty, and the pursuit of happiness. The **Declaration of Independence** was **adopted** on July 4, 1776. July 4th in the United States is **Independence Day**.

Las colonias no estaban conformes con que Inglaterra las gobernara. Por eso, Thomas Jefferson escribió la **Declaración de Independencia**. La Declaración dijo que las colonias querían ser libres de Inglaterra. La **creeencia fundamental** es que todos los hombres fueron creados iguales. Dice que todos tienen derecho a la vida, la libertad y la busca de felicidad. La **Declaración de Independencia** fue adoptada el 4 de julio de 1776. Desde entonces, en los Estados Unidos el 4 de julio es el **Día de independencia**.

Declaration of Independence
- written by Thomas Jefferson
- says that all men are created equal
- Affirms the principles of life, liberty, and the pursuit of happiness
- stated that the colonies were independent of England
- adopted on July 4, 1776

Declaración de Independencia
- escrita por Thomas Jefferson
- declara que todos los hombres fueron creados iguales
- Afirma los principales de la vida, la libertad y la busca de felicidad
- declara que las colonias querían ser libres de Inglaterra
- adoptada el 4 de julio de 1776

✪ Repetition / Repetición

Repeat these questions and answers out loud. / Repite estas preguntas y respuestas en voz alta.

1. What is the 4th of July?
Independence Day

2. When was the Declaration of Independence adopted?
July 4, 1776

3. What is the basic belief of the Declaration of Independence?
All men are created equal.

4. What important rights are listed in the Declaration of Independence?
Life, liberty, and the pursuit of happiness

5. Who was the main writer of the Declaration of Independence?
Thomas Jefferson

6. What else did the Declaration say?
The colonies were free from England

✪ Exercises / Ejercicios

Los ejercicios siguientes han sido diseñados para familiarizarte con el material de esta lección. El verdadero examen de ciudadanía puede ser oral o un examen de respuestas múltiples.

Multiple-choice questions / Preguntas de opción múltiple

The following exercises have been designed to familiarize you with the material of this lesson. The actual citizenship test may be oral or written. / Marca las respuestas a las preguntas siguientes. Las respuestas a estos ejercicios se encuentran en la última página de esta lección.

1. (a) (b) (c) (d)   4. (a) (b) (c) (d)

2. (a) (b) (c) (d)   5. (a) (b) (c) (d)

3. (a) (b) (c) (d)

1. When was the Declaration of Independence adopted?
   a. 1776
   b. 1777
   c. 1789
   d. 1787

2. What is the basic belief of the Declaration of Independence?
   a. all men should fight in an army
   b. all men are created equal
   c. the president has absolute power
   d. only citizens can live in United States

3. Who was the main writer of the Declaration of Independence?
   a. Abraham Lincoln
   b. Bill Clinton
   c. Thomas Jefferson
   d. George Washington

4. What is the date of Independence Day?
   a. June 4th
   b. December 25th
   c. July 1st
   d. July 4th

5. Which of the following rights is NOT promised in the Declaration of Independence?
   a. life
   b. wealth
   c. liberty
   d. happiness

Circle the correct answer / Encierra en un círculo la respuesta correcta.

1. The Declaration of Independence was adopted on _____, 1776.
July 4   December 25

2. The basic belief of the Declaration of Independence is _____.
United States comes first   all men are created equal

3. _____ Day is on the 4th of July.
Independence   Memorial

4. The main writer of the Declaration of Independence was _____.
George Washington   Thomas Jefferson

5. The Declaration said that the colonies were free from _____.
slavery   England

"Yes" or "no" questions / Preguntas de "sí" o "no"

Yes   No   The 4th of July is Independence Day.

Yes   No   The basic belief of the Declaration of Independence is that all men are created equal.

Yes   No   The Declaration of Independence made the colonies free from England.

Yes   No   The main writer of the Declaration of Independence was George Washington.

Yes   No   The Declaration of Independence was written in 1787.

Yes   No   The basic belief of the Declaration of Independence is that the President should have absolute power.

Yes   No   The Declaration of Independence was adopted on July 4, 1776.

Yes   No   The main writer of the Declaration of Independence was Thomas Jefferson.

✪ Dictation Practice / Práctica de dictado

Write each sentence twice. The first time, copy it. The second time, don't look at it. Have someone read it aloud while you write it. / Escribe cada oración dos veces. La primera vez, cópiala. La segunda vez, haz que alguien lea la oración mientras la escribes.

1. The woman is eating.

2. She is eating an apple.

3. I see that the woman is eating an apple.

1. _____.

1. _____.

2. _____.

2. _____.

3. _____.

3. _____.

✪ Lesson 15 Answers / Respuestas de la Lección 15

Multiple-choice questions / Preguntas de opción múltiple
1. a. 1776
2. b. all men are created equal
3. c. Thomas Jefferson
4. d. July 4th
5. d. Independence Day
6. b. wealth

Circle the correct answer / Encierra en un círculo la respuesta correcta.

1. The Declaration of Independence was adopted on _____, 1776.
   (July 4)   December 25

2. The basic belief of the Declaration of Independence is _____.
   United States comes first   (all men are created equal)

3. _____ Day is on the 4th of July.
   (Independence)   Memorial

4. The main writer of the Declaration of Independence was _____.
   George Washington   (Thomas Jefferson)

5. The Declaration said that the colonies were free from _____.
   slavery   (England)

"Yes" or "no" questions / Preguntas de "sí" o "no"

(Yes) No   The 4th of July is Independence Day.

(Yes) No   The basic belief of the Declaration of Independence is that all men are created equal.

(Yes) No   The Declaration of Independence made the colonies free from England.

Yes **(No)**   The main writer of the Declaration of Independence was George Washington.

Yes **(No)**   The Declaration of Independence was written in 1787.

Yes **(No)**   The basic belief of the Declaration of Independence is that the President should have absolute power.

(Yes) No   The Declaration of Independence was adopted on July 4, 1776.

(Yes) No   The main writer of the Declaration of Independence was Thomas Jefferson.

Review Quiz 5 / Prueba de repaso 5

Mark the answers for each question on this sheet. The correct answers can be found on the last page of the quiz. / Marca las respuestas a las preguntas siguientes. Las respuestas correctas se encuentran en la última página de la prueba de repaso.

1. (a)   (b)   (c)   (d)   6. (a)   (b)   (c)   (d)

2. (a)   (b)   (c)   (d)   7. (a)   (b)   (c)   (d)

3. (a)   (b)   (c)   (d)   8. (a)   (b)   (c)   (d)

4. (a)   (b)   (c)   (d)   9. (a)   (b)   (c)   (d)

5. (a)   (b)   (c)   (d)

1. Why did the Pilgrims come to America?
   a. to pay taxes
   b. religious freedom
   c. farmland
   d. to escape war

2. What holiday was first celebrated by the American colonists?
   a. Christmas
   b. Halloween
   c. Labor Day
   d. Thanksgiving

3. Who helped the Pilgrims in America?
   a. Native Americans
   b. colonists
   c. slaves
   d. King George

4. Who was the main writer of the Declaration of Independence?
   a. George Washington
   b. Benjamin Franklin
   c. Abraham Lincoln
   d. Thomas Jefferson

5. When was the Declaration of Independence written?
   a. July 4, 1778
   b. July 4, 1776
   c. July 4, 1787
   d. July 4, 1620

6. What is the basic belief of the Declaration of Independence?
   a. the president has absolute power
   b. only citizens can vote
   c. all men are created equal
   d. only citizens can live in the United States

7. What rights does the Declaration of Independence emphasize?
   a. life, liberty, and the pursuit of happiness
   b. freedom of speech, freedom of the press, freedom of religion
   c. freedom from paying taxes
   d. the right to bear arms

8. What were the 13 original states called?
   a. colonies
   b. territories
   c. provinces
   d. settlements

9. Which of these states was a colony?
   a. California
   b. Washington
   c. Minnesota
   d. New York

Review Quiz 5 Answers / Respuestas de la prueba de repaso 5

1. b. religious freedom
2. d. Thanksgiving
3. a. Native Americans
4. d. Thomas Jefferson
5. b. July 4, 1776
6. c. all men are created equal
7. a. colonies
8. d. New York
9. a. life, liberty, and the pursuit of happiness

Lesson 16 / Lección 16

The Revolutionary War and George Washington / La Guerra Revolucionaria y George Washington

✪ Words to Know / Palabras claves

independence:	freedom (independencia)
liberty:	freedom (libertad)
Revolutionary War:	war between the 13 colonies and England (guerra entre las colonias e Inglaterra)

✪ About the Revolutionary War and George Washington / Sobre la Guerra Revolucionaria y George Washington

During the **Revolutionary War**, the United States fought England to gain **independence**. The colonists were led by the first commander in chief of the U.S. military, George Washington. The war lasted from 1775 to 1783. The United States won and gained **independence** from England. After the **Revolutionary War**, George Washington was the first president elected by the people in the United States. He is called the "father of our country."

Durante la **Guerra Revolucionaria** los Estados Unidos peleó contra Inglaterra para poder obtener su **independencia**. Los colonizadores fueron dirigidos por el primer comandante en jefe de las fuerzas armadas estadounidenses, George Washington. Los Estados Unidos ganó su **independencia** de Inglaterra. Después de la **Guerra Revolucionaria,** George Washington fue elegido por la gente de los Estados Unidos como primer presidente. Se conoce como "el padre de nuestro país".

Revolutionary War

- The United States fought England to gain independence.
- colonists led by George Washington.
- George Washington became president after the war.

La Guerra Revolucionaria

- los Estados Unidos peleó contra Inglaterra para ganar su independencia.
- los colonizadores fueron dirigidos por George Washington.
- George Washington llegó a ser presidente después de la guerra.

✪ Repetition / Repetición

Repeat these questions and answers out loud. / Repite estas preguntas y respuestas en voz alta.

1. Which president was the first commander in chief of the U.S. military?
George Washington

2. Who did the United States gain independence from?
England

3. Who was the first president elected by the people in the United States?
George Washington

4. Which president is called the "father of our country"?
George Washington

✪ Exercises / Ejercicios

Los ejercicios siguientes han sido diseñados para familiarizarte con el material de esta lección. El verdadero examen de ciudadanía puede ser oral o un examen de respuestas múltiples.

Multiple-choice questions / Preguntas de opción múltiple
The following exercises have been designed to familiarize you with the material of this lesson. The actual citizenship test may be oral or written. / Marca las respuestas a las preguntas siguientes. Las respuestas a estos ejercicios se encuentran en la última página de esta lección.

1. ⓐ ⓑ ⓒ ⓓ   3. ⓐ ⓑ ⓒ ⓓ

2. ⓐ ⓑ ⓒ ⓓ   4. ⓐ ⓑ ⓒ ⓓ

1. Who did the United States gain independence from?
   a. England
   b. France
   c. Spain
   d. Mexico

2. Who is called the "father of our country"?
   a. Abraham Lincoln
   b. George Washington
   c. John Hancock
   d. Thomas Jefferson

3. Which president was the first commander in chief of the U.S. military?
   a. George W. Bush
   b. Abraham Lincoln
   c. George Washington
   d. Thomas Jefferson

4. Why did the Revolutionary War happen?

    a. The colonists did not have freedom of religion and wanted to protest.

    b. The colonists wanted to invade and conquer England.

    c. The colonists were angry because they paid taxes without being represented in the English government.

    d. The colonists wanted George Washington to be king.

Circle the correct answer / Encierra en un círculo la respuesta correcta.

1. _____ was the first commander in chief of the U.S. military.

    George Washington   Thomas Jefferson

2. The United States gained independence from _____.

    England   France

3. The United States fought _____ during the Revolutionary War.

    England   France

4. _____ was the first president elected by the people in the United States.

    George Washington   Thomas Jefferson

5. George Washington is called the "_____ of our country."

    father   brother

"Yes" or "no" questions / Preguntas de "sí" o "no"

Yes   No   George Washington was the first commander in chief of the U.S. military.

Yes   No   United States fought France during the Revolutionary War.

Yes   No   The United States gained independence from England.

Yes   No   George Washington is called the "father of our country."

Yes   No   United States fought England during the Revolutionary War.

Yes   No   George Washington was the first president elected by the people.

✪ Dictation Practice / Práctica de dictado

Write each sentence twice. The first time, copy it. The second time, don't look at it. Have someone read it aloud while you write it. / Escribe cada oración dos veces. La primera vez, cópiala. La segunda vez, haz que alguien lea la oración mientras la escribes.

1. I have a cat.

2. I have had my cat four years.

3. My cat has lived with me for four years.

1. _____.

1. _____.

2. _____.

2. _____.

3. _____.

3. _____.

✪ Lesson 16 Answers / Respuestas de la Lección 16

Multiple-choice questions / Preguntas de opción múltiple

1. a. England
2. b. George Washington
3. c. George Washington
4. c. The colonists were angry because they paid taxes without being represented in the English government.
5. a. George Washington
6. c. England

Circle the correct answer / Encierra en un círculo la respuesta correcta.

1. _____ was the first commander in chief of the U.S. military.
   (George Washington)   Thomas Jefferson

2. The U.S. gained independence from _____.
   (England)   France

3. The United States fought _____ during the Revolutionary War.
   (England)   France

4. _____ was the first president elected by the people in the United States.
   (George Washington)   Thomas Jefferson

5. George Washington is called the "_____ of our country."
   (father)   brother

"Yes" or "no" questions / Preguntas de "sí" o "no"

(Yes) No George Washington was the first commander in chief of the U.S. military.

Yes **(No)** The United States fought France during the Revolutionary War.

(Yes) No The United States gained independence from England.

(Yes) No George Washington is called the "father of our country."

(Yes) No The United States fought England during the Revolutionary War.

(Yes) No Patrick Henry said, "Give me liberty or give me death."

(Yes) No George Washington was the first president elected by the people.

Lesson 17 / Lección 17

The Civil War / La Guerra Civil

✪ Words to Know / Palabras claves

Civil War: war between the North and South (Guerra Civil)

slave: someone who is owned by another person (esclavo)

✪ About the Civil War / Sobre la Guerra Civil

After the Revolutionary War and the Constitution, the country became bigger. In 1800, the United States purchased the **Louisiana Territory** from France. From 1861 to 1865, there was a war between states in the North and states in the South. It was called the **Civil War** because it was fought between states in the same country. Several states in the South wanted to start their own country. They didn't want to be a part of the United States. The North wanted all the states to stay together but without slavery. One reason for the **Civil War** was slavery. Many people in the South owned **slaves**. Many people in the North were against slavery. The North won the war, and that is why there is no more slavery in the United States.

Después de la Guerra Revolucionaria y la Constitución, el país creció. En 1800, los Estados Unidos compró el **Territorio de Louisiana** de Francia. De 1861 a 1865, hubo una guerra entre los estados del Norte y los del Sur. Se llama la **Guerra Civil** porque fue peleada entre estados del mismo país. Muchos estados en el Sur querían formar su propia nación. Ya no querían ser parte de los Estados Unidos. El Norte quería que todos los estados se mantuvieran unidos pero sin esclavitud. Una razón por la **Guerra Civil** fue la esclavitud. Muchas personas del Sur eran dueñas. Muchas personas del Norte se oponían a la esclavitud. El Norte ganó la guerra, y por eso ya no hay esclavitud en los Estados Unidos.

The Civil War
- The North opposed slavery.
- The South supported slavery.
- The South wanted to be their own country
- Slavery tore the country apart.

La Guerra Civil
- El Norte se oponía a la esclavitud.
- El Sur apoyaba la esclavitud.
- El Sur quería formar su propia nación.
- La esclavitud fue la causa que dividió el país en dos partes.

- War lasted from 1861 to 1865.
- The North won the war.

- La guerra duró de 1861 a 1865.
- El Norte ganó la guerra.

✪ Repetition / Repetición

Repeat these questions and answers out loud. / Repite estas preguntas y respuestas en voz alta.

1. What was one of the reasons for the Civil War?
slavery

2. Who wanted to start their own country?
the South

3. Who wanted the states to stay together?
the North

4. When did the Civil War take place?
from 1861 to 1865

5. Who won the Civil War?
the North

✪ Exercises / Ejercicios

Los ejercicios siguientes han sido diseñados para familiarizarte con el material de esta lección. El verdadero examen de ciudadanía puede ser oral o un examen de respuestas múltiples.

Multiple-choice questions / Preguntas de opción múltiple

The following exercises have been designed to familiarize you with the material of this lesson. The actual citizenship test may be oral or written. / Marca las respuestas a las preguntas siguientes. Las respuestas a estos ejercicios se encuentran en la última página de esta lección.

1. ⓐ   ⓑ   ⓒ   ⓓ   **4.** ⓐ   ⓑ   ⓒ   ⓓ

2. ⓐ   ⓑ   ⓒ   ⓓ   **5.** ⓐ   ⓑ   ⓒ   ⓓ

3. ⓐ   ⓑ   ⓒ   ⓓ

1. Who wanted the states to stay together?
   a. the South
   b. the North
   c. the West
   d. the East

2. One reason for the Civil War was
   a. freedom of the seas.
   b. taxes.
   c. slavery.
   d. religious freedom.

3. Who fought during the Civil War?
   a. East and West
   b. West and East
   c. West and North
   d. North and South

4. Who wanted to start their own country?
   a. the South
   b. the North
   c. the West
   d. the East

5. Who won the Civil War?
   a. the South
   b. the North
   c. the East
   d. the West

Circle the correct answer / Encierra en un círculo la respuesta correcta.

1. _____ wanted to start their own country.
   The North   The South

2. During the Civil War the _____ fought.
   North/South   East/West

3. _____ was one reason for the Civil War.
   Slavery   Taxes

4. The North wanted the states to stay _____.
   together   apart

5. The _____ won the Civil War.
   South   North

"Yes" or "no" questions / Preguntas de "sí" o "no"

Yes	No	The East and West fought during the Civil War.
Yes	No	The South wanted to start their own country.
Yes	No	The Civil War ended in 1865.
Yes	No	The North wanted the states to stay together.
Yes	No	The North and South fought during the Civil War.
Yes	No	One reason for the Civil War was slavery.
Yes	No	The North won the Civil War.

✪ Dictation Practice / Práctica de dictado

Write each sentence twice. The first time, copy it. The second time, don't look at it. Have someone read it aloud while you write it. / Escribe cada oración dos veces. La primera vez, cópiala. La segunda vez, haz que alguien lea la oración mientras la escribes.

1. I wear a hat.

2. I wear a yellow hat.

3. I wear hats.

1. _____ .

1. _____ .

2. _____ .

2. _____ .

3. _____ .

3. _____ .

⊙ Lesson 17 Answers / Respuestas de la Lección 17

Multiple-choice questions / Preguntas de opción múltiple
1. b. the North
2. c. slavery
3. d. North and South
4. a. the South
5. b. the North

Circle the correct answer / Encierra en un círculo la respuesta correcta.

1. _____ wanted to start their own country.
   The North   (The South)

2. During the Civil War the _____ fought.
   (North/South)   East/West

3. _____ was one reason for the Civil War.
   (Slavery)   Taxes

4. The North wanted the states to stay _____.
   (together)   apart

5. The _____ won the Civil War.
   South   (North)

"Yes" or "no" questions / Preguntas de "sí" o "no"

Yes   (No)   The East and West fought during the Civil War.

(Yes)   No   The South wanted to start their own country.

(Yes)   No   The Civil War ended in 1865.

(Yes)   No   The North wanted the states to stay together.

(Yes)   No   The North and South fought during the Civil War.

(Yes)   No   One reason for the Civil War was slavery.

(Yes)   No   The North won the Civil War.

Lesson 18 / Lección 18

Abraham Lincoln and the Emancipation Proclamation / Abraham Lincoln y la Proclamación de Emancipación

✪ Words to Know / Palabras claves

Emancipation Proclamation: written statement that freed the slaves (Proclamación de emancipación)

united: stay together as one (unídos)

✪ About Abraham Lincoln / Sobre Abraham Lincoln

Abraham Lincoln was president during the Civil War. He wanted the country to be **united**, and he was against slavery. President Lincoln freed the slaves by writing the **Emancipation Proclamation** in 1863. After the war, the **Emancipation Proclamation** became the 13th amendment to the Constitution.

Durante la Guerra Civil, Abraham Lincoln fue el presidente. El se oponía a la esclavitud y quería que el país estuviera **unido**. El presidente Lincoln liberó a los esclavos con un escrito llamado la **Proclamación de Emancipación**. Después de la Guerra la **Proclamación de Emancipación** llegó a ser la enmienda número 13 de la Constitución.

Abraham Lincoln
- president during Civil War
- against slavery
- wrote the Emancipation Proclamation to end slavery

Abraham Lincoln
- presidente durante la Guerra Civil
- en contra de la esclavitud
- escribió la Proclamación de Emancipación para poner término a la esclavitud

✪ Repetition / Repetición

Repeat these questions and answers out loud. / Repite estas preguntas y respuestas en voz alta.

1. Who was the president during the Civil War?
Abraham Lincoln

2. What did the Emancipation Proclamation do?
freed many slaves

3. Which president freed the slaves?
Abraham Lincoln

4. What freed the slaves?
Emancipation Proclamation

✪ Exercises / Ejercicios

Los ejercicios siguientes han sido diseñados para familiarizarte con el material de esta lección. El verdadero examen de ciudadanía puede ser oral o un examen de respuestas múltiples.

Multiple-choice questions / Preguntas de opción múltiple
The following exercises have been designed to familiarize you with the material of this lesson. The actual citizenship test may be oral or written. / Marca las respuestas a las preguntas siguientes. Las respuestas a estos ejercicios se encuentran en la última página de esta lección.

1. ⓐ ⓑ ⓒ ⓓ   **3.** ⓐ ⓑ ⓒ ⓓ

2. ⓐ ⓑ ⓒ ⓓ   **4.** ⓐ ⓑ ⓒ ⓓ

1. Who freed the slaves?
   a. President Lincoln
   b. the Supreme Court
   c. President Jefferson
   d. President Washington

2. Who was president during the Civil War?
   a. Abraham Lincoln
   b. George Washington
   c. Bill Clinton
   d. Thomas Jefferson

3. What did the Emancipation Proclamation do?
   a. freed the slaves
   b. freed the women
   c. purchased land
   d. expanded the country

4. In what year were the slaves freed?
   a. 1861
   b. 1865
   c. 1863
   d. 1787

Circle the correct answer / Encierra en un círculo la respuesta correcta.

1. President _____ freed the slaves.
   Washington   Lincoln

2. Abraham Lincoln was _____ during the Civil War.
   president   a slave

3. The Emancipation Proclamation freed the _____.
   slaves   colonists

4. The _____ won the Civil War.
   South   North

"Yes" or "no" questions / Preguntas de "sí" o "no"

Yes   No   George Washington was president during the Civil War.

Yes   No   President Lincoln freed the slaves.

Yes   No   The Emancipation Proclamation freed the slaves.

Yes   No   Abraham Lincoln was president during the Civil War.

Yes   No   The slaves were freed by the Emancipation Proclamation.

Yes   No   The Emancipation Proclamation was written in 1865.

✪ Dictation Practice / Práctica de dictado

Write each sentence twice. The first time, copy it. The second time, don't look at it. Have someone read it aloud while you write it. / Escribe cada oración dos veces. La primera vez, cópiala. La segunda vez, haz que alguien lea la oración mientras la escribes.

1. I am learning English.

2. They are learning English.

3. My sisters are learning English.

1. _____.

1. _____.

2. _____.

2. _____.

3. _____.

3. _____.

✪ Lesson 18 Answers / Respuestas de la Lección 18

Multiple-choice questions / Preguntas de opción múltiple
1. a. President Lincoln
2. a. Abraham Lincoln
3. a. freed the slaves
4. b. the Emancipation Proclamation

Circle the correct answer / Encierra en un círculo la respuesta correcta.

1. President _____ freed the slaves.
   Washington   (Lincoln)

2. Abraham Lincoln was _____ during the Civil War.
   (president)   a slave

3. The Emancipation Proclamation freed the _____.
   (slaves)   colonists

4. The _____ won the Civil War.
   South   (North)

"Yes" or "no" questions / Preguntas de "sí" o "no"

Yes   (No)   George Washington was president during the Civil War.

(Yes)   No   President Lincoln freed the slaves.

(Yes)   No   The Emancipation Proclamation freed the slaves.

(Yes)   No   Abraham Lincoln was president during the Civil War.

(Yes)   No   The slaves were freed by the Emancipation Proclamation.

Yes   (No)   The Emancipation Proclamation was written in 1865.

Lesson 19 / Lección 19

History after the Civil War / Historia después de la Guerra Civil

✪ Words to Know / Palabras claves

allies:
friends during wartime (aliados)

Civil Rights Movement:
A movement seeking rights, justice, and social equality (un movimiento que buscaba los derechos, la justicia, y la igualdad social para todos)

Cold War:
A conflict between the United States and Soviet Union that was a struggle between capitalism and communism (un conflicto entre los Estados Unidos y la Unión Soviética que representaba una lucha entre el capitalismo y el comunismo)

✪ Some Events in Later History / Unos sucesos de la historia reciente

By the twentieth century, the United States had become a major force on the world stage. From 1914 to 1918, the United States fought in World War I. Woodrow Wilson was the president at this time. America's role in World War II established our country as a world leader. America and its allies fought against Germany, Italy, and Japan, and helped to win the war in 1945. Franklin Delano Roosevelt, or FDR, was the president during this war. Eisenhower, who later became president, was a general during this war.

Durante el siglo XX, los Estados Unidos llegaba a ser una fuerza mayor en el mundo. Desde 1914 hasta 1918, los Estados Unidos luchó en World War I. Woodrow Wilson fue el presidente en este tiempo. Las acciones de los Estados Unidos durante World War II establecieron nuestro país como un líder mundial. Los Estados Unidos y sus aliados pelearon contra Alemania, Italia, y el Japón y ganaron la guerra in 1945. Franklin Delano Roosevelt (FDR) fue el presidente durante esta guerra. Eisenhower, quien después

From the 1950s to 1990s, the United States participated in a Cold War against the Soviet Union, which was a struggle against communism, and it also fought wars in Korea (the Korean War) and Vietnam (the Vietnam War).

In the 1960s, the Civil Rights movement fought for the rights of groups that had been treated unfairly. Dr. Martin Luther King, Jr., fought for the equality of all Americans, and 100 years before him, Susan B. Anthony struggled for the rights of women.

On September 11, 2001, a great tragedy occurred as terrorists attacked the United States.

llegó a ser presidente, fue un general durante este conflicto. Desde los 1950s hasta los 1990s, los Estados Unidos participó en una Guerra Fría contra la Unión Soviética, que era una pelea contra el comunismo, y también luchó en guerras en Corea (la Guerra Coreana) y Viet Nam (la Guerra de Viet Nam).

En los 1960s, el movimiento de los derechos civiles luchó por los derechos de los grupos que habían sido mal tratados. Dr. Martin Luther King, Jr., peleó por la igualdad de todos los estadounidenses, y cien años antes de él, Susan B. Anthony peleó por los derechos de los mujeres.

El 11 de septiembre de 2001, una gran tragedia ocurrió cuando unos terroristas atacaron a los Estados Unidos.

✪ Repetition / Repetición

Repeat these questions and answers out loud. / Repite estas preguntas y respuestas en voz alta.

1. Who were the United States's enemies in World War II?
Germany, Italy, and Japan

2. What did Susan B. Anthony do?
fought for women's right to vote

3. Who led the United States during WWI?
Woodrow Wilson

4. What war did Eisenhower fight in?
World War II

5. What was the United States fighting against during the Cold War?
communism

6. Who was Martin Luther King, Jr.?
a civil rights leader

✪ Exercises / Ejercicios

Los ejercicios siguientes han sido diseñados para familiarizarte con el material de esta lección. El verdadero examen de ciudadanía puede ser oral o un examen de respuestas múltiples.

Multiple-choice questions / Preguntas de opción múltiple

The following exercises have been designed to familiarize you with the material of this lesson. The actual citizenship test may be oral or written. / Marca las respuestas a las preguntas siguientes. Las respuestas a estos ejercicios se encuentran en la última página de esta lección.

1. ⓐ ⓑ ⓒ ⓓ   **4.** ⓐ ⓑ ⓒ ⓓ

2. ⓐ ⓑ ⓒ ⓓ   **5.** ⓐ ⓑ ⓒ ⓓ

3. ⓐ ⓑ ⓒ ⓓ   **6.** ⓐ ⓑ ⓒ ⓓ

1. Who was president during WWII?
   a. Woodrow Wilson
   b. George Washington
   c. Franklin D. Roosevelt
   d. Abraham Lincoln

2. What general in World War II later became president?
   a. Wilson
   b. Eisenhower
   c. Clinton
   d. Powell

3. Who were the United States's enemies in World War II?
   a. Germany, Italy, and Japan
   b. Canada, Russia, and Poland
   c. Mexico and Brazil
   d. Britain and France

4. Which person fought for the rights of women?
   a. Susan B. Anthony
   b. Martin Luther King, Jr.
   c. Thomas Jefferson
   d. Patrick Henry

5. Who was Martin Luther King, Jr.?
   a. a civil rights leader
   b. the president
   c. a senator
   d. a tax collector

6. What happened on September 11, 2001?
   a. The United States became independent from England.
   b. The North won the Civil War.
   c. The Civil Rights movement began.
   d. Terrorists attacked the United States.

Circle the correct answer / Encierra en un círculo la respuesta correcta.

1. Who were two of the United States's enemies in World War II?
   Britain/Canada   Japan/Italy

2. Who was president during World War I?
   Wilson   Eisenhower

3. When did terrorists attack the United States?
   September 11, 2001   July 4, 1776

4. What did the United States fight against in the Cold War?
   terrorism   communism

5. Which wars did the United States fight during the twentieth century?
   Revolutionary War and Civil War   Korean War and Vietnam War

6. Who was a civil rights leader?
   Martin Luther King, Jr.   Francis Scott Key

"Yes" or "no" questions / Preguntas de "sí" o "no"

Yes   No   Germany and Japan were two of the United States's enemies in World War II.

Yes   No   Martin Luther King, Jr. was a civil rights leader.

Yes   No   Martin Luther King, Jr., was a congressman.

Yes   No   Susan B. Anthony fought for women's rights.

Yes   No   The Civil Rights movement fought for lower taxes.

Yes   No   Eisenhower was a general and a president.

Yes   No   September 11, 2001, was an uneventful day in the country's history.

✪ Dictation Practice / Práctica de dictado

Write each sentence twice. The first time, copy it. The second time, don't look at it. Have someone read it aloud while you write it. / Escribe cada oración dos veces. La primera vez, cópiala. La segunda vez, haz que alguien lea la oración mientras la escribes.

1. I like snow.

2. Today it is snowing.

3. The snow is cold.

1. _____.

1. _____.

2. _____.

2. _____.

3. _____.

3. _____.

⊙ Lesson 19 Answers / Respuestas de la Lección 19

Multiple-choice questions / Preguntas de opción múltiple
1. c. Franklin D. Roosevelt
2. b. Eisenhower
3. a. Germany, Italy, and Japan
4. a. Susan B. Anthony
5. a. a civil rights leader
6. d. Terrorists attacked the United States.

Circle the correct answer / Encierra en un círculo la respuesta correcta.

1. Who were two of the United States's enemies in World War II?
   Britain/Canada   (Japan/Italy)

2. Who was president during World War I?
   (Wilson)   Eisenhower

3. When did terrorists attack the United States?
   (September 11, 2001)   July 4, 1776

4. What did the United States fight against in the Cold War?
   terrorism   (communism)

5. Which wars did the United States fight during the 20th century?
   Revolutionary War and Civil War   (Korean War and Vietnam War)

6. Who was a civil rights leader?
   (Martin Luther King, Jr.)   Francis Scott Key

"Yes" or "no" questions / Preguntas de "sí" o "no"

(Yes)   No   Germany and Japan were two of the United States's enemies in World War II.

(Yes)   No   Martin Luther King, Jr. was a civil rights leader.

Yes   (No)   Martin Luther King, Jr., was a congressman.

(Yes)   No   Susan B. Anthony fought for women's rights.

Yes   (No)   The Civil Rights movement fought for lower taxes.

(Yes)   No   Eisenhower was a general and a president.

Yes   (No)   September 11, 2001 was a happy day in the country's history.

Lesson 20 / Lección 20

The United States Today /
Los Estados Unidos actuales

✪ Words to Know / Palabras claves

democracy: government of, by, and for the people (gobierno de, por y para la gente)

Democratic Republic: the form of the U.S. government (república democrática)

political party: group with similar ideas about government (partido político)

Capitalism: the economic system of the United States based on free markets (el sistema económico de los Estados Unidos que es basado en los mercados libres)

✪ About the United States Today / Sobre los Estados Unidos actuales

In the United States today, there are 50 states. The capital of the United States is in Washington, D.C. The two major **political parties** in the U.S. are the Democrats and Republicans. The government of the United States is a **democratic republic**, which Abraham Lincoln called a "government of the people, by the people, and for the people." A government where the people decide who the leaders will be is called a **democracy**.

En los Estados Unidos hay 50 estados. La capital de los Estados Unidos es Washington, D.C. Los dos **partidos políticos** más importantes de los Estados Unidos son los Demócratos y los Republicanos. El gobierno de los Estados Unidos es una **república democrática,** a la cual Abraham Lincoln llamó un "gobierno de la gente, por la gente y para la gente". Un sistema en que la gente decide quiénes serán sus líderes se llama **democracia**.

United States Today	Los Estados Unidos actualmente
■ 50 states	■ 50 estados
■ two political parties (Republican, Democrat)	■ dos partidos políticos (republicano, demócrata)
■ democratic republic	■ república democrática
■ capitalism	■ capitalismo

✪ Repetition / Repetición

Repeat these questions and answers out loud. / Repite estas preguntas y respuestas en voz alta.

1. How many states are in the United States?
50

2. Where is the capital of the United States?
Washington, D.C.

3. What are the two major political parties in the United States?
Democrat and Republican

4. What kind of government does the United States have?
democratic republic

5. What kind of economic system does the United States have?
capitalism

✪ Exercises / Ejercicios

Los ejercicios siguientes han sido diseñados para familiarizarte con el material de esta lección. El verdadero examen de ciudadanía puede ser oral o un examen de respuestas múltiples.

Multiple-choice questions / Preguntas de opción múltiple

The following exercises have been designed to familiarize you with the material of this lesson. The actual citizenship test may be oral or written. / Marca las respuestas a las preguntas siguientes. Las respuestas a estos ejercicios se encuentran en la última página de esta lección.

1. ⓐ　ⓑ　ⓒ　ⓓ　　**3.** ⓐ　ⓑ　ⓒ　ⓓ

2. ⓐ　ⓑ　ⓒ　ⓓ　　**4.** ⓐ　ⓑ　ⓒ　ⓓ

1. Where is the capital of the United States?
   a. New York City
   b. Washington, D.C.
   c. Philadelphia, PA
   d. Los Angeles

2. What kind of government does the United States have?
   a. democratic republic
   b. feudalism
   c. communist
   d. republic of states

3. How many states are in the union?
   a. 13
   b. 48
   c. 50
   d. 52

4. What are the two major political parties in the United States?
   a. Democrat and Republican
   b. Communist and Fascist
   c. Judicial and Republican
   d. Executive and Democratic

Circle the correct answer / Encierra en un círculo la respuesta correcta.

1. Democrat and Republican are the two major _____ in the United States.
political parties   companies

2. There are _____ states in the United States.
50   13

3. _____ and Republican are the two major political parties in the United States.
Congress   Democrat

4. The United States government is a _____.
monarchy   democratic republic

5. The capital of the United States is in _____.
New York City   Washington, D.C.

"Yes" or "no" questions / Preguntas de "sí" o "no"

Yes No The capital of the United States is in New York City.

Yes No Our government is a democratic republic.

Yes No There are 50 states in the United States.

Yes No Democrat and Republican are the two major political parties in the United States.

Yes No The United States has a communist form of government.

Yes No The capital of the United States is in Washington, D.C.

Yes No Our government is of the people, by the people, and for the people.

Yes No The United States has a socialist economic system.

✪ Dictation Practice / Práctica de dictado

Write each sentence twice. The first time, copy it. The second time, don't look at it. Have someone read it aloud while you write it. / Escribe cada oración dos veces. La primera vez, cópiala. La segunda vez, haz que alguien lea la oración mientras la escribes.

1. The child plays with a truck.

2. The child plays with a toy.

3. The child's favorite toy is a truck.

1. _____.

1. _____.

2. _____.

2. _____.

3. _____.

3. _____.

✪ Lesson 20 Answers / Respuestas de la Lección 20

Multiple-choice questions / Preguntas de opción múltiple
1. b. Washington, D.C.
2. a. democratic republic
3. c. 50
4. a. Democrat and Republican

Circle the correct answer / Encierra en un círculo la respuesta correcta.

1. Democrat and Republican are the two major _____ in the United States.
   (political parties)   companies

2. There are _____ states in the United States.
   (50)   13

3. _____ and Republican are the two major political parties in the United States.
   Congress   (Democrat)

4. The United States government is a _____.
   monarchy   (democratic republic)

5. The capital of the United States is in _____.
   New York City   (Washington, D.C.)

"Yes" or "no" questions / Preguntas de "sí" o "no"

Yes   (No)   The capital of the United States is in New York City.

(Yes)   No   Our government is a democratic republic.

(Yes)   No   There are 50 states in the United States.

(Yes)   No   Democrat and Republican are the two major political parties in the United States.

Yes   (No)   The United States has a communist form of government.

(Yes)   No   The capital of the United States is in Washington, D.C.

(Yes)   No   Our government is of the people, by the people, and for the people.

Yes   (No)   The United States has a socialist economic system.

Lesson 21 / Lección 21

Symbols and Geography / Los símbolos y la geografía

✪ Words to Know / Palabras claves

Atlantic Ocean:　　Ocean that borders the United States on its east coast (el océano que está en la costa oriental de los Estados Unidos)

Mississippi River:　　The longest river in the United States (el río más largo de los Estados Unidos)

✪ About Symbols and Geography / Sobre los símbolos y la geografía

The United States has a flag that is red, white, and blue. There are 50 white stars that **represent** the 50 states in the union. There are 13 red and white stripes that **represent** the original thirteen colonies. Our **National Anthem** is about the flag. The name of our **National Anthem** is "The Star-Spangled **Banner**," and it was written by Francis Scott Key.

Another important symbol of the United States is the Statue of Liberty, which is located in New York Harbor.

The United States borders Canada to the north and Mexico to the south, and it is in between the Atlantic Ocean on its East Coast and the Pacific Ocean on its West Coast. Some states that border Canada are Maine, Minnesota, and Wisconsin, and some states that border Mexico are Texas, Arizona, and California. The country is made up of 50 states and five territories. The territories include

La bandera de los Estados Unidos es de color rojo, blanco y azul. Tiene cincuenta estrellas blancas que **representan** los cincuenta estados y trece franjas rojas y blancas que **representan** las trece colonias originales. Nuestro himno nacional trata de la bandera. El nombre de nuestro **himno nacional** es "The Star-Spangled **Banner**," ("La **bandera** adornada de estrellas"), y fue escrita por Francis Scott Key.

Otro símbolo importante de los Estados Unidos es la Estatua de la Libertad, que está en Nueva York.

Los Estados Unidos limitan al norte con el Canadá y con México al sur, y está entre Océano Atlántico al este y la Océano Pacífico al oeste. Algunos estados que limitan a Canadá son Maine, Minnesota y Wisconsin, y algunos estados que limitan a México son Texas, Arizona y California. La nación se compone de 50

Puerto Rico, Guam, and American Samoa. Every state has a capital, and the capital of the country is Washington, D.C. The longest river in the United States is the Mississippi, and the tallest mountain is Mt. McKinley.

The U.S. Flag
- red, white, and blue
- 50 stars (for the 50 states)
- 13 stripes (for the original colonies)

The National Anthem
- written about the U.S. flag
- written by Francis Scott Key

Geography
- 50 states and 5 territories
- Mississippi River, Mt. McKinley
- Statue of Liberty in New York

estados y cinco territorios. Los territorios incluyen a Puerto Rico, Guam y Samoa Americana. Cada estado tiene una capital, y la capital de la nación es Washington, D.C. El río más largo del país es el Mississippi, y la montaña más alta es Mt. McKinley.

La bandera de los Estados Unidos
- rojo, blanco y azul
- 50 estrellas (por los 50 estados)
- 13 franjas (por las primeras colonias)

El himno nacional
- se refiere a la bandera de los Estados Unidos
- escrita por Francis Scott Key

La geografía
- 50 estados y 5 territorios
- El río Mississippi y el monte McKinley
- la Estatua de la Libertad en New York

✪ Repetition / Repetición

Repeat these questions and answers out loud. / Repite estas preguntas y respuestas en voz alta.

1. What are the colors of our flag?
red, white, and blue

2. How many stars are on our flag?
50 (fifty)

3. What color are the stars on our flag?
white

4. What do the stars on the flag represent?
The 50 (fifty) states. There is one star for each state in the union.

5. How many stripes are on the flag?
13 (thirteen)

6. What color are the stripes?
red and white

7. What do the stripes on the flag represent?
the original 13 (thirteen) colonies

8. What is the national anthem of the United States?
"The Star-Spangled Banner"

9. Where is the Statue of Liberty located?
in New York Harbor

10. What is a state that borders Canada?
Minnesota, Maine, New York, Minnesota, North Dakota, Montana, Washington

✪ Exercises / Ejercicios

Los ejercicios siguientes han sido diseñados para familiarizarte con el material de esta lección. El verdadero examen de ciudadanía puede ser oral o un examen de respuestas múltiples.

Multiple-choice questions / Preguntas de opción múltiple

The following exercises have been designed to familiarize you with the material of this lesson. The actual citizenship test may be oral or written. / Marca las respuestas a las preguntas siguientes. Las respuestas a estos ejercicios se encuentran en la última página de esta lección.

1. (a) (b) (c) (d)   **6.** (a) (b) (c) (d)

2. (a) (b) (c) (d)   **7.** (a) (b) (c) (d)

3. (a) (b) (c) (d)   **8.** (a) (b) (c) (d)

4. (a) (b) (c) (d)   **9.** (a) (b) (c) (d)

5. (a) (b) (c) (d)

1. How many stars are on the flag?
    a. 13
    b. 42
    c. 50
    d. 52

2. What are the colors of our flag?
   a. red, white, and blue
   b. blue, orange, and red
   c. red, white, and pink
   d. red, white, and green

3. How many stripes are on the flag?
   a. 10
   b. 13
   c. 50
   d. 52

4. What color are the stars on the flag?
   a. red
   b. white
   c. blue
   d. black

5. What do the stripes on the flag represent?
   a. the 50 states
   b. the original 13 colonies
   c. the House of Representatives
   d. the Civil War

6. What do the stars on the flag represent?
   a. the 50 states
   b. Alaska and Hawaii
   c. Francis Scott Key
   d. the Pilgrims

7. What is the national anthem of the United States?
   a. "The Star-Spangled Banner"
   b. "My Country"
   c. "America the Beautiful"
   d. "Let the Eagle Soar"

8. Where is the Statue of Liberty?
   a. New York City
   b. San Francisco
   c. Washington, D.C.
   d. Philadelphia

9. Which of the following states does not border Mexico?
   a. Texas
   b. Arizona
   c. Kansas
   d. California

Matching questions / Preguntas para emparejar

Answer each question with the appropriate letter from the right column. / Relaciona cada pregunta con la letra más apropiada de la columna derecha.

_____ What do the stripes on the flag represent?	A.	red, white, and blue
_____ What color are the stripes?	B.	50
_____ What color are the stars on the flag?	C.	white
_____ How many stripes are on the flag?	D.	50 states
_____ What do the stars on the flag represent?	E.	13
_____ What are the colors of our flag?	F.	red and white
_____ How many stars are on the flag?	G.	the 13 original colonies
_____ What is the national anthem of the United States?	H.	"The Star-Spangled Banner"

"Yes" or "no" questions / Preguntas de "sí" o "no"

Yes   No   The stars on the flag are white.

Yes   No   The flag is red, white, and blue.

Yes   No   The stripes on the flag represent the 13 original colonies.

Yes   No   The flag has 50 stripes on it.

Yes   No   The stripes on the flag are red and white.

Yes   No   The stars on the flag represent the 50 stars in the sky.

Yes   No   The stars on the flag are blue.

Yes   No   "The Star-Spangled Banner" is the national anthem of the United States.

Yes   No   The flag has 50 stars on it.

✪ Dictation Practice / Práctica de dictado

Write each sentence twice. The first time, copy it. The second time, don't look at it. Have someone read it aloud while you write it. / Escribe cada oración dos veces. La primera vez, cópiala. La segunda vez, haz que alguien lea la oración mientras la escribes.

1. I can read English.

2. I can write English.

3. I can read, write, and speak English.

1. _____ .

1. _____ .

2. _____ .

2. _____ .

3. _____ .

3. _____ .

Multiple-choice questions / Preguntas de opción múltiple

1. c. 50
2. a. red, white, and blue
3. b. 13
4. b. white
5. b. original 13 colonies
6. a. 50 states
7. a. "The Star-Spangled Banner"
8. a. New York City
9. c. Kansas

Preguntas para agrupar

_G_ What do the stripes on the flag represent?
_F_ What color are the stripes?
_C_ What color are the stars on the flag?
_E_ How many stripes are on the flag?
_D_ What do the stars on the flag represent?
_A_ What are the colors of our flag?
_B_ How many stars are on the flag?
_H_ What is the national anthem of the United States?

A. red, white, and blue
B. 50
C. white
D. 50 states
E. 13
F. red and white
G. original 13 colonies
H. "The Star-Spangled Banner"

"Yes" or "no" questions / Preguntas de "sí" o "no"

(Yes) No The stars on the flag are white.

(Yes) No The flag is red, white and blue.

(Yes) No The stripes on the flag represent the original 13 colonies.

Yes (No) The flag has 50 stripes on it.

(Yes) No The stripes on the flag are red and white.

Yes (No) The stars on the flag represent the 50 stars in the sky.

Yes (No) The stars on the flag are blue.

(Yes) No "The Star-Spangled Banner" is the national anthem of the United States.

(Yes) No The flag has 50 stars on it.

Lesson 22 / Lección 22

State and Local Governments / Gobiernos locales y estatales

✪ Words to Know / Palabras claves

capital: city where the government is located (ciudad donde se encuentra el gobierno)

✪ About State and Local Governments / Sobre los gobiernos estatales y locales

Each state has its own **capital**. You need to know what the **capital** of your state is. For example, the **capital** of Texas is Austin, the **capital** of New York state is Albany, and the capital of Florida is Tallahassee. Every state has a governor as its head executive. Each state also has two senators who represent that state in Washington, D.C. Within each state are many local governments. Each city has a mayor as its head executive.

Cada estado tiene su propia **capital**. Es preciso saber cuál es la **capital** de tu estado. Por ejemplo, la **capital** de Texas es Austin, la **capital** del estado de Nueva York es Albany y la capital de Florida es Tallahassee. El jefe del ejecutivo de cada estado es el gobernador. Cada estado tiene también dos senadores que lo representan en Washington, D.C. Dentro de cada estado hay muchos gobiernos locales. El jefe del ejecutivo de una ciudad es el alcalde.

State Government

- The government is located in the capital city.
- The governor is the head executive.
- Two (2) senators represent each state in Washington, D.C.

Gobierno estatal

- La capital es donde se encuentra el gobierno.
- El gobernador es el jefe del ejecutivo.
- Dos (2) senadores representan cada estado en Washington, D.C.

Local Government

- The mayor is head executive of every city.
- There are many local governments in each state.

Gobierno local

- El alcalde es el jefe del ejecutivo de una ciudad.
- Hoy muchos gobiernos locales en cada estado.

✪ Repetition / Repetición

Repeat these questions and answers out loud. / Repite estas preguntas y respuestas en voz alta.

1. What is the capital of your state? _____

2. Who is the current governor of your state? _____

3. Who are the two senators from your state? _____

4. Who is the head of your local government? _____

5. What are some important powers that state governments have?_____

✪ Exercises / Ejercicios

Los ejercicios siguientes han sido diseñados para familiarizarte con el material de esta lección. El verdadero examen de ciudadanía puede ser oral o un examen de respuestas múltiples.

Circle the correct answer / Encierra en un círculo la respuesta correcta.

Pregunta a un maestro o a un familiar las respuestas a las preguntas siguientes. Si no puedes encontrar la respuesta a una de estas preguntas, anda a la biblioteca pública y pregunta al bibliotecario. Escribe las respuestas que encuentres en los espacios en blanco que siguen.

1. The head of my local government is _____.

2. _____ is the capital of my state.

3. The governor of my state is _____.

4. The two senators from my state are _____ and _____.

5. _____ is the mayor of my city.

Copia los oraciones

Copia dos veces cada oración que sigue después de que hayas llenado los espacios vacíos.

1. The head of my local government is _____.

_____.

_____.

2. The governor of my state is _____.

_____.

_____.

3. The two senators from my state are _____ and _____.

_____.

_____.

✪ Dictation Practice / Práctica de dictado

Write each sentence twice. The first time, copy it. The second time, don't look at it. Have someone read it aloud while you write it. / Escribe cada oración dos veces. La primera vez, cópiala. La segunda vez, haz que alguien lea la oración mientras la escribes.

1. Today is Tuesday.

2. Tomorrow is Wednesday.

3. Today it is windy.

1. _____ .

1. _____ .

2. _____ .

2. _____ .

3. _____ .

3. _____ .

Lesson 23 / Lección 23

American Citizens / Ciudadanos estadounidenses

✪ Words to Know / Palabras claves

benefits: rewards or advantages (beneficios)

minimum: the lowest number allowed (mínimo)

responsibilities: things that people must do (responsabilidades)

✪ About American Citizens / Sobre ciudadanos estadounidenses

The most important right granted to U.S. citizens is the right to vote. The **minimum** voting age in the United States is 18. The amendments to the Constitution that guarantee or discuss voting rights are the 15th, 19th, 24th, and the 26th. There are many **benefits** to becoming a U.S. citizen, such as the right to travel with a U.S. passport, the right to serve on a jury, and the right to apply for federal jobs. The USCIS form used to apply to become a naturalized citizen is Form N-400 "Application for Naturalization."

The **right to vote** is the single most important right of U.S. citizens, and it is reserved for citizens.

Citizens also have important responsibilities, which include voting, serving on a jury, paying income taxes by April 15, and registering for the selective service (for men of age 18). When you become a citizen you give your allegiance to the

El derecho más importante que se otorga a los ciudadanos estadounidenses (americanos), es el derecho de votar. La edad **mínima** para votar en los Estados Unidos es 18 años. La enmiendas a la Constitución que garantizan o tratan de los derechos al voto son 15ta, 19na, 24ta y 26ta. Hay muchos **beneficios** al convertirte en ciudadano estadounidense: el derecho al voto, el derecho de viajar con un pasaporte estadounidense, el derecho de servir como jurado y el derecho de solicitar empleos federales. El formulario del USCIS que se usa para solicitar la ciudadanía naturalizada es el Form N-400 "*Application for Naturalization*" (Solicitud para naturalización).

El **derecho de votar** es el derecho más importante de los ciudadanos de los Estados Unidos, y se reserva solamente para los ciudadanos.

Los ciudadanos también tienen unas responsabilidades importantes, incluyendo votar, servir en un jurado, pagar los

country, which is symbolized by the **Pledge of Allegiance.**

impuestos federales antes de 15 de abril, y registrar para el Servicio Selectivo (para los hombres de más de 18 años de edad). Cuando llegue a ser ciudadano, dará su alianza al país, que es simbolizada por la **Prenda de Alianza.**

Voting

- The minimum voting age is 18.
- The 15th, 19th, 24th, and the 26th amendments to the Constitution discuss voting.

Voto

- La edad mínima para votar es 18 años.
- Los 15ta, 19na, 24ta y 26na enmiendas a la Constitución tratan del derecho al voto.

Benefits of Citizenship

- right to vote
- right to travel with a U.S. passport
- right to serve on a jury
- right to apply for federal jobs

Beneficios de la ciudadanía

- derecho al voto
- derecho de viajar con pasaporte estadounidense
- derecho de servir como jurado
- derecho de solicitar empleo federal

✪ Repetition / Repetición

Repeat these questions and answers out loud. / Repite estas preguntas y respuestas en voz alta.

1. What is the most important right granted to U.S. citizens?
   the right to vote

2. What is the minimum voting age in the United States?
   18 (eighteen)

3. What do the amendments governing voting rights say about who can vote?
   Men and women can vote; people of any race can vote; people over 18 can vote; no one has to pay to vote.

4. What are some ways in which you can become involved in the democracy around you?
   Vote; write to your congressman; serve on a jury; join a political party.

5. Who do you give your allegiance to when you say the Pledge of Allegiance?
to the country, or to the flag

6. What are some of the benefits to becoming a United States citizen?
right to vote, right to travel with a U.S. passport, right to serve on a jury, right to apply for federal jobs

7. What USCIS form is used to apply to become a naturalized citizen?
N-400 "Application for Naturalization"

✪ Exercises / Ejercicios

Los ejercicios siguientes han sido diseñados para familiarizarte con el material de esta lección. El verdadero examen de ciudadanía puede ser oral o un examen de respuestas múltiples.

Multiple-choice questions / Preguntas de opción múltiple

The following exercises have been designed to familiarize you with the material of this lesson. The actual citizenship test may be oral or written. / Marca las respuestas a las preguntas siguientes. Las respuestas a estos ejercicios se encuentran en la última página de esta lección.

1. ⓐ   ⓑ   ⓒ   ⓓ   **4.** ⓐ   ⓑ   ⓒ   ⓓ

2. ⓐ   ⓑ   ⓒ   ⓓ   **5.** ⓐ   ⓑ   ⓒ   ⓓ

3. ⓐ   ⓑ   ⓒ   ⓓ   **6.** ⓐ   ⓑ   ⓒ   ⓓ

1. Which of the following is a benefit of becoming a U.S. citizen?
   a. right to pay taxes
   b. right to vote
   c. right to go to school
   d. right to work in federal job

2. The Constitution does NOT give the right to vote to which of the following groups?
   a. women citizens
   b. citizens over the age of 18
   c. citizens of any race
   d. permanent residents

3. Which of the following is NOT something you must do when you become a citizen?
   a. become loyal to the United States
   b. give up your loyalty to other places
   c. memorize the Constitution
   d. serve the United States

4. What is the minimum voting age in the United States?
   a. 16
   b. 18
   c. 21
   d. 25

5. What is the most important right granted to U.S. citizens?
   a. right to work
   b. right to apply for federal jobs
   c. right to an education
   d. right to vote

6. What USCIS form is used to apply to become a naturalized citizen?
   a. N-200 "Petition for Naturalization"
   b. N-400 "Application for Naturalization"
   c. Social Security Card
   d. Form 1040

Circle the correct answer / Encierra en un círculo la respuesta correcta.

1. What is one responsibility that only citizens have?
   obey the law   serve on a jury

2. What is the most important right granted to U.S. citizens?
   right to work   right to vote

3. What is the minimum voting age in the United States?
   16   18

4. What is a benefit of becoming a U.S. citizen?
   right to travel with a U.S. passport   right to own a home

5. What USCIS form is used to apply to become a naturalized citizen?
   N-400 "Application for Naturalization"   N-200 "Petition for Naturalization"

"Yes" or "no" questions / Preguntas de "sí" o "no"

Yes   No   The minimum voting age in the United States is 21.

Yes   No   The right to vote is the most important right granted to U.S. citizens.

Yes   No   The right to bear arms is the most important right granted to U.S. citizens.

Yes   No   Eighteen is the minimum voting age in the United States.

Yes   No   Federal income taxes are due on April 15.

Yes   No   All men and women must register for the Selective Service.

Yes   No   The Pledge of Allegiance is a statement of loyalty to the country.

Yes   No   Being a citizen includes both important rights and responsibilities.

✪ Dictation Practice / Práctica de dictado

Write each sentence twice. The first time, copy it. The second time, don't look at it. Have someone read it aloud while you write it. / Escribe cada oración dos veces. La primera vez, cópiala. La segunda vez, haz que alguien lea la oración mientras la escribes.

1. It is sunny.

2. It is cold outside.

3. It is sunny but cold today.

1. _____.

1. _____.

2. _____.

2. _____.

3. _____.

3. _____.

Multiple-choice questions / Preguntas de opción múltiple

1. b. right to vote
2. c. memorize the Constitution
3. b. 18
4. d. right to vote
5. b. N-400 "Application for Naturalization"

Circle the correct answer / Encierra en un círculo la respuesta correcta.

1. What is one responsibility that only citizens have?
obey the law   (serve on a jury)

2. What is the most important right granted to U.S. citizens?
right to work   (right to vote)

3. What is the minimum voting age in the United States?
16   (18)

4. What is a benefit of becoming a U.S. citizen?
right to own a home   (right to travel with a U.S. passport)

5. What USCIS form is used to apply to become a naturalized citizen?
(N-400 "Application for Naturalization")   N-200 "Petition for Naturalization"

"Yes" or "no" questions / Preguntas de "sí" o "no"

Yes (No) The minimum voting age in the United States is 21.

(Yes) No The right to vote is the most important right granted to U.S. citizens.

Yes (No) The right to bear arms is the most important right granted to U.S. citizens.

(Yes) No Eighteen is the minimum voting age in the United States.

(Yes) No Federal income taxes are due on April 15.

Yes (No) All men and women must register for the Selective Service.

(Yes) No The Pledge of Allegiance is a statement of loyalty to the country.

(Yes) No Being a citizen involves important rights as well as responsibilities.

Review Quiz 6 / Prueba de repaso 6

Mark the answers for each question on this sheet. The correct answers can be found on the last page of the quiz. / Marca las respuestas a las siguientes preguntas. Las respuestas correctas se encuentran en la última página de la prueba de repaso.

1. (a) (b) (c) (d)   9. (a) (b) (c) (d)

2. (a) (b) (c) (d)   10. (a) (b) (c) (d)

3. (a) (b) (c) (d)   11. (a) (b) (c) (d)

4. (a) (b) (c) (d)   12. (a) (b) (c) (d)

5. (a) (b) (c) (d)   13. (a) (b) (c) (d)

6. (a) (b) (c) (d)   14. (a) (b) (c) (d)

7. (a) (b) (c) (d)   15. (a) (b) (c) (d)

8. (a) (b) (c) (d)

1. How many senators does your state have?
   a. one
   b. two
   c. three
   d. four

2. Which countries were our enemies during World War II?
   a. Mexico, Canada, England
   b. Spain, Italy, France
   c. Russia, France, England
   d. Germany, Italy, Japan

3. Who was Martin Luther King, Jr.?
   a. commander in chief
   b. a Supreme Court justice
   c. a civil rights leader
   d. a senator

4. What is the minimum voting age in the United States?
   a. 17
   b. 16
   c. 21
   d. 18

5. What is the most important right granted to U.S. citizens?
   a. the right to vote
   b. the right to bear arms
   c. the right to travel
   d. the right to work

6. How many states are in the union?
   a. thirteen
   b. forty
   c. forty-eight
   d. fifty

7. What are the two main political parties in the United States?
   a. Communist and Fascist
   b. Democrat and Republican
   c. Partisan and Democratic
   d. Judicial and Republican

8. What form of government does the United States have?
   a. democratic republic
   b. socialist republic
   c. monarchy
   d. civil union

9. What are the colors of our flag?
  a. red, white, and blue
  b. blue, orange, and red
  c. red, white, and pink
  d. red, white, and green

10. How many stripes are on the flag?
  a. 10
  b. 13
  c. 50
  d. 52

11. What do the stripes on the flag represent?
  a. the 50 states
  b. the 13 original colonies
  c. the *Mayflower*
  d. the Pilgrims

12. What do the stars on the flag represent?
  a. the 50 states
  b. the 13 original colonies
  c. the Revolutionary War
  d. The Bill of Rights

13. What is the longest river in the United States?
  a. the Mississippi
  b. the Missouri
  c. the Chattahoochee
  d. the Ohio

14. What is the economic system used in the United States today?
  a. socialism
  b. barter
  c. capitalism
  d. centrally planned

15. Which of the following rights is NOT exclusively for citizens?
  a. the right to vote
  b. the right to a fair trial
  c. the right to serve on a jury
  d. the right to carry a U.S. passport

Review Quiz 6 Answers / Respuestas de la prueba de repaso 6

1. b. two
2. d. Germany, Italy, Japan
3. c. a civil rights leader
4. d. 18
5. a. the right to vote
6. d. 50
7. b. Democrat and Republican
8. a. democratic republic
9. a. red, white, and blue
10. b. 13
11. b. the 13 original colonies
12. a. the 50 states
13. a. the Mississippi
14. c. capitalism
15. b. the right to a fair trial

CAPÍTULO 5

Palabras claves para estudiar

✪ Civics and History Glossary / Glosario de civismo e historia

This list contains important terms for citizenship and their definitions. Study the list and try to understand what each term means and how it relates to American history and civics. The key terms are in English; the definitions appear in both Spanish and English.

Esta lista contiene términos y definiciones importantes para lograr la ciudadanía. Estudia la lista para entender lo que significa cada palabra y como se vincula con la historia y el gobierno de los Estados Unidos. Las palabras claves están en inglés; las definiciones se expresan en español e inglés.

adopted	put into effect; *hecho entrar en vigor*
advises	gives help to; *da consejo*
affiliated	linked or connected; *afiliados*
allies	friends during wartime; *aliados*
amendments	changes or additions to the Constitution; *enmiendas*
appointed	chosen or selected; *nombrado*

banner	flag; *bandera*
basic belief	main idea, most important part; *creencia fundamental*
bear arms	carry a gun; *llevar armas*
benefits	rewards or advantages; *beneficios*
Bill of Rights	the first ten amendment to the Constitution; *Declaración de Derechos*
branches	separate parts; *ramas*
Cabinet	fourteen (14) people who help the president make decisions; *gabinete*
capital	city where the government is located; *ciudad donde se encuentra el gobierno*
Capitol	where Congress meets; *edificio donde se reúne el Congreso*
checks and balances	separation of powers that keeps one branch of the government from becoming too powerful; *la separación de poderes que previene que una rama del gobierno llegue a ser demasiado poderosa*
chief justice	head of the Supreme Court; *juez principal*
civil rights leader	person who promotes justice for all races of people; *persona que ayuda a otros a creer en la justicia para toda la gente de todas las razas*
Civil War	war between the North and South; *Guerra Civil*
colonies	original 13 states in United States; *13 estados originales de los Estados Unidos*
Congress	people who make our laws; *gente que hace nuestras leyes*
Constitution	the supreme law of the United States; *ley suprema de los Estados Unidos*
Declaration of Independence	written statement saying the colonies wanted to be free; *declaración escrita que estableció que las colonias querían ser independientes de Inglaterra*
democracy	government of, by, and for the people; *gobierno de, por y para la gente*

Democratic Republic	the form of the U.S. government; *república democrática*
Electoral College	group who elects the president; *grupo que elige al presidente*
Emancipation Proclamation	written statement that freed the slaves; *Proclamación de Emancipación*
enemies	people we fought against; *enemigos*
executive branch	part of government made up of the president, vice president, and cabinet; *rama ejecutiva*
Federalist Papers	Documents written by Hamilton, Madison, and Jay that supported the passage of the Constitution; *unos documentos escritos por Hamilton, Madison y Jay que sostenían el pasaje de la Constitución.*
governor	leader of a state; *gobernador*
head executive	the leader or person in charge; *jefe del ejecutivo*
inaugurated	sworn into office; *puesto en oficina a través de un juramento*
Independence Day	July 4th; *el 4 de Julio, el Día de Independencia*
independence	freedom; *independencia*
interpret	to explain; *interpretar, explicar*
introduction	the first part; *introducción*
judicial branch	the part of the government that includes the Supreme Court; *parte del gobierno que incluye la Corte Suprema*
King George	King of England who ruled over the colonies; *el rey de Inglaterra que gubernaba las colonias*

legislative branch	Congress; *Congreso*
liberty	freedom; *libertad*
mayor	leader of a city; *alcalde*
minimum	the lowest number allowed; *mínimo*
National Anthem	song about United States; *canción acerca de los Estados Unidos*
Native Americans	people living in America when the Pilgrims arrived; *americanos indígenos*
natural-born citizen	person born in a country; *una persona que nace en un país*
Pledge of Allegiance	official statement that you will help the United States; *juramento de fidelidad*
Pilgrims	people who came from England on a ship called the Mayflower; *Peregrinos*
political party	group with similar ideas about government; *partido político*
preamble	the introduction to the Constitution; *preámbulo*
re-elected	voted into office again; *reelegido*
representatives	people who work in the House of Representatives; *representantes que hacen las leyes*
responsibilities	things that people must do; *responsabilidades*
Revolutionary War	war between the 13 colonies and England; *guerra entre las colonias e Inglaterra*
Rule of Law	The idea that everyone must follow the law and no one is above the law; *la idea que nadie está sobre la ley y todos tienen que obedecerla*

senators	people who work in the Senate making laws; *senadores*
slave	someone who is owned by another person; *esclavo*
Supreme Court	highest court in the United States; *Corte Suprema*
supreme law	the highest, most important law; *la ley más alta y más importante*
term	how long someone works in government; *duración de trabajo en el gobierno*
Thanksgiving	a holiday that was first celebrated by the Pilgrims and the Native Americans; *Día de acción de gracias*
the union	all the states of United States; *todos los estados de los Estados Unidos*
tried	put through a trial with a judge and jury; *juzgado*
union	*los Estados Unidos*
united	stay together as one; *unidos*
White House	home of the president; *casa donde vive el presidente*

✪ Interview Glossary / Glosario de entrevista

This list contains useful terms for your interview with the USCIS official. Study the list to understand what each term means. The key terms are in English; the definitions appear in both Spanish and English.

Esta lista contiene términos útiles para tu entrevista con el oficial del USCIS. Estudia la lista para entender el significado de cada palabra. Las palabras claves están en inglés; las definiciones se expresan en español e inglés.

address	where you live; *donde vives, dirección*
alien	foreigner; *extranjero*
arrested	formally charged of a crime by a police officer; *arrestado*
birthplace	country where you were born; *lugar de nacimiento*
born	*nacido*

citizenship	the right to fully participate in the benefits and laws of the country where you live; *ciudadanía*
communist	person who belongs to a party that supports common ownership of production and distribution of products; *comunista*
conscientious objections	reasons a person refuses to fight in a war; *razones por las cuales una persona se niega a pelear en una guerra*
crime	an illegal action; *crimen*
deported	ordered by a judge to leave the country; *deportado*
desert	leave the military without permission; *desertar*
drafted	chosen to be a soldier; *elegido para ser soldado*
employer	the company or person you work for; *empleador, patrón*
exemption	permission to stay out of; *exención*
false testimony	to lie before a judge; *mentir ante un juez*
habitual drunkard	person who drinks too much alcohol; *borracho*
illegal drugs	narcotics, cocaine, marijuana, dope, speed; *drogas ilegales*
illegal gambling	to play cards for money; *apostar o jugarse ilegalmente*
income tax	the money you pay to the government if you work in the United States; *impuesto sobre la renta*
incompetent	insane or unable to function alone; *loco o incapaz de vivir solo*
job	work of duty; *trabajo*
laid off	fired; *despedido*

maiden name	a woman's last name before getting married; *apellido de soltera*
marital status	whether you are single, married, or divorced; *estado civil*
mental institution	hospital for people whose minds do not work; *manicomio*
nobility	of royal blood; *nobleza*
noncombatant service	helping the military without fighting; *trabajar con los militares sin pelear en la guerra*
oath	promise to tell the truth; *juramento*
Oath of Allegiance	official statement that you will help the United States; *juramento de fidelidad*
occupation	job; *trabajo*
persecution	hurting someone because of their race, religion, national origin, or political opinion; *persecución*
polygamy	having more than one husband or one wife at the same time; *poligamia*
port of entry	place where you arrived in the country; *puerto de entrada*
prostitute	person who has sex for money; *prostituto*
registered	officially signed up; *registrado*
smuggling	illegally sneaking someone or something into the country; *contrabandar*

CAPÍTULO 6

Historia y civismo: Toda la información que requiere oficialmente el USCIS

Over the course of this book, you have learned about American history and civics. You have learned the answers to the questions in this chapter. These 100 questions comprise the entire body of information that might appear on your citizenship test. Study these questions and you will be very prepared for the test!

A través del libro has estudiado la historia y civismo estadounidenses. Ya has aprendido las respuestas que corresponden a las preguntas de este capítulo. Estas 100 preguntas representan toda la información que puede incluir el examen de ciudadanía. ¡Estudia estas preguntas y estarás muy bien preparado para el examen!

✪ The structure of the U.S. government/La estructura del gobierno de los Estados Unidos

1. Name one branch or part of the government.

1. executive, legislative, judicial (president, Congress, Supreme Court)

2. What stops one branch from becoming too powerful?

2. checks and balances

✪ The Legislative Branch/La rama legislativa

3. Who makes federal laws?

3. Congress

4. What are the two parts of Congress?

4. Senate and House of Representatives

5. How many senators are there?

5. 100

6. How long is a senator's term?

6. six years

7. Who is one of your state's senators?

7. pregunta a un profesor, o a un familiar la respuesta a esta pregunta

8. How many voting members are in the House of Representatives?

8. 435

9. We elect representatives for how many years?

9. two years

10. Who is your U.S. representative?

10. pregunta a un profesor, o a un familiar la respuesta a esta pregunta

11. Who does a U.S. senator represent?

11. all the people of the state

12. Why do some states have more representatives than others?

12. number depends on population

✪ The Judicial Branch/La rama judicial

13. What does the judicial branch do?

13. reviews or explains laws, settles disputes, determines if laws are constitutional

14. What is the highest court in the United States?

14. the Supreme Court

15. How many justices are on the Supreme Court?

15. nine justices

16. Who is the Chief Justice of the United States?

16. John Roberts

✪ The Executive Branch/La rama ejecutiva

17.	Who is in charge of the executive branch?	**17.**	the president
18.	We elect a president for how many years?	**18.**	four years
19.	In what month do we vote for the president?	**19.**	November
20.	In what month is the president inaugurated?	**20.**	January
21.	Who is the president of the United States now?	**21.**	George W. Bush
22.	Who is the Vice President of the United States now?	**22.**	Dick (Richard) Cheney
23.	If the president can no longer serve, who becomes president?	**23.**	the vice president
24.	If the president and vice president can both no longer serve, who becomes president?	**24.**	The speaker of the House of Representatives
25.	Who is the commander in chief of the military?	**25.**	the president
26.	Who signs bills to make them laws?	**26.**	the president
27.	Who vetoes bills?	**27.**	the president
28.	What does the president's cabinet do?	**28.**	advises the president
29.	What are two cabinet-level positions?	**29.**	many responses, including secretary of defense, secretary of state, secretary of labor, secretary of the treasury, secretary of agriculture

✪ The Constitution/La Constitución

30.	What is the supreme law of the land?	**30.**	the Constitution
31.	What does the Constitution do?	**31.**	sets up the government and protects rights of citizens
32.	The idea of self-government comes from the first three words of the Constitution. What are they?	**32.**	"We the People"
33.	What is an amendment?	**33.**	a change to the Constitution
34.	What do we call the first ten amendments to the Constitution?	**34.**	the Bill of Rights
35.	What is one right or freedom from the First Amendment?	**35.**	freedom of speech; freedom of religion; freedom of the press

36. How many amendments does the Constitution have?

37. What did the Declaration of Independence do?

38. What are two rights in the Declaration of Independence?

39. What is freedom of religion?

40. What is the rule of law?

41. Under the Constitution, the federal government has certain powers. Name one.

42. The Constitution gives state governments certain rights. Name one.

36. 27 amendments

37. declared American independence from England

38. life, liberty, the pursuit of happiness

39. the freedom to practice any religion or no religion at all

40. the idea that no one is above the law; everyone must follow the law

41. collect taxes, raise an army, sign treaties

42. provide education, police, fire departments

✪ The History of the United States/La historia de los Estados Unidos

43. What is one reason colonists came to America?

44. Who lived in America before the Europeans arrived?

45. Name one Native American tribe.

46. What group of people was taken to America and sold as slaves?

47. Why did the colonists fight the English?

48. Who wrote the Declaration of Independence?

49. When was the Declaration of Independence adopted?

50. There were 13 original states. Name one.

43. freedom, freedom of religion

44. Native Americans

45. many answers, including Cherokee, Sioux, Creek, Apache, Navajo

46. Africans

47. because they paid high taxes and were not represented in government

48. Thomas Jefferson

49. July 4, 1776

50. New Hampshire, Massachusetts, Connecticut, Rhode Island, New York,

---

51. What happened at the Constitutional Convention?
52. When was the Constitution written?
53. The Federalist Papers supported the passage of the Constitution. Name one of the writers.
54. What is one thing Benjamin Franklin is famous for?

55. Who is the father of our country?
56. Who was the first president?
57. What territory did the United States buy from France in 1803?
58. Name one war fought by the United States during the 1800s.
59. Name the United States war between North and South.
60. Name one problem that led to the Civil War.
61. What was one important thing that Abraham Lincoln did?

62. What did the Emancipation Proclamation do?
63. What did Susan B. Anthony do?
64. Name one war fought by the United States during the 1900s.

65. Who was president during World War I?
66. Who was president during the Great Depression and World War II?

New Jersey, Pennsylvania, Delaware, Maryland, Virginia, North Carolina, South Carolina, Georgia
51. the Constitution was written
52. in 1776
53. Alexander Hamilton, James Madison, John Jay
54. oldest member of the Constitutional Convention, author of Poor Richard's Almanac, U.S. diplomat

55. George Washington
56. George Washington
57. Louisiana

58. War of 1812, Civil War

59. the Civil War

60. slavery, states' rights

61. signed the Emancipation Proclamation, led the United States through the Civil War, preserved the union
62. freed the slaves

63. fought for women's rights
64. World War I, World War II, Vietnam War, Korean War

65. Woodrow Wilson
66. Franklin D. Roosevelt (FDR)

67. Who did the United States fight in World War II?

68. Before he was President, Eisenhower was a general. What war was he in?

69. During the Cold War, what was the main concern of the United States?

70. What movement tried to end racial discrimination?

71. What did Martin Luther King, Jr., do?

72. What major event happened on September 11, 2001?

67. Germany, Japan, and Italy

68. World War II

69. defeating communism

70. the Civil Rights movement

71. fought for civil rights (equal rights for all Americans)

72. Terrorists attacked the United States.

✪ Symbols and Geography/Los símbolos y la geografía

73. Why does the flag have 13 stripes?

74. Why does the flag have 50 stars?

75. What is the name of the national anthem?

76. Name one of the two longest rivers in the United States

77. What ocean is on the West Coast of the United States?

78. What ocean is on the East Coast of the United States?

79. Name one U.S. territory.

80. Name one state that borders Canada.

81. Name one state that borders Mexico.

82. What is the capital of the United States?

83. Where is the Statue of Liberty located?

73. to represent 13 original colonies

74. to represent 50 states

75. "The Star-Spangled Banner"

76. Mississippi, Missouri

77. the Pacific Ocean

78. the Atlantic Ocean

79. Guam, Puerto Rico, U.S. Virgin Islands, American Samoa

80. Many answers, including Maine, New Hampshire, Vermont, Michigan, Minnesota, Montana

81. Texas, Arizona, New Mexico, California

82. Washington, D.C.

83. New York Harbor

✪ Your State Government/El gobierno de tu estado

84. Who is the governor of your state?

85. What is the capital of your state?

84. Pregunta a un profesor, o a un familiar la respuesta a esta pregunta.

85. Pregunta a un profesor, o a un familiar la respuesta a esta pregunta.

✪ The United States Today/Los Estados Unidos actuales

86. There are four amendments to the Constitution about who can vote. Name one.

86. People of any race can vote, women can vote; people over 18 can vote; you don't have to pay to vote.

87. What is one responsibility that is only for U.S. citizens?

87. voting, serving on a jury

88. What are two rights only for U.S. citizens?

88. voting, applying for a federal job, carrying a passport

89. What are the rights of everyone in the United States?

89. freedom of expression, freedom of speech, freedom of religion, right to bear arms

90. What do we show loyalty to when we say the Pledge of Allegiance?

90. the flag of the United States

91. What is one promise you make when you become a U.S. citizen?

91. to give up loyalties to other countries; to serve the United States; to defend the Constitution

92. How old do citizens have to be to vote for president?

92. 18 years of age

93. What are two ways Americans can participate in their democracy?

93. Vote, join a political party, run for office, write to a newspaper

94. When is the last day to send in income tax forms?

94. April 15

95. When must all men register for the Selective Service?

95. at age 18

96. What are the two major political parties in the United States?

96. Democrats and Republicans

97. What is the political party of the president now?

97. Republican

98. What is the name of the speaker of the House of Representatives now?

98. Nancy Pelosi

99. When do we celebrate Independence Day?

99. July 4

100. Name two national holidays.

100. Many responses including: Independence Day, Labor Day, Memorial Day, Thanksgiving

CAPÍTULO 7

Preguntas de práctica: Entrevista y formulario N-400

This is a list of sample questions that you might be asked in your interview with the USCIS official or on the N-400 form. Be prepared to answer these questions based on your own personal information. Also, you may notice that some groups of questions ask for the same information in different ways. It is important to be able to recognize this. Have someone read the questions to you aloud, then answer out loud.

Esto es una lista de preguntas que pueden aparecer durante tu entrevista con el oficial del USCIS o en el formulario N-400. Prepárate a contestar estas preguntas según tu información personal. También verás que algunos grupos de preguntas piden la misma información aunque de manera distinta. Lee con cuidado. Pide que alguien te lea las preguntas y contéstalas en voz alta.

Question:	Do you understand what an oath is?
Answer:	Yes, it is a promise to tell the truth.
Question:	What is your complete name?
Answer:	My name is Yolanda Rodríguez Martínez.
Question:	What is your name?
Answer:	Yolanda Rodríguez Martínez.

Question: What is your address?
Answer: My address is 423 Tenth Avenue, Brooklyn, New York 55555.

Question: Where do you live?
Answer: I live at 423 Tenth Avenue, Brooklyn, New York 55555.

Question: What is your home phone number?
Answer: My home phone number is 718-555-7889.

Question: What is your telephone number at home?
Answer: It is 718-555-7889.

Question: Do you have a work telephone number?
Answer: Yes, my work number is 212-555-6000.

Question: What is your work phone number?
Answer: My work phone number is 212-555-6000.

Question: Do you have a work number?
Answer: No, I am not currently working.

Question: May I see your passport?
Answer: Yes, here it is.

Question: Do you have your passport with you?
Answer: Yes, I do.

Question: What is your current citizenship?
Answer: I am currently a citizen of Mexico.

Question: Where do you come from?
Answer: I come from Mexico.

Question: What is your date of birth?
Answer: July 12, 1953.

Question: When were you born?
Answer: I was born on July 12, 1953.

Question: What is your birth date?
Answer: My birth date is July 12, 1953.

Question: Where were you born?
Answer: I was born in India.

Question: What is your place of birth?
Answer: India.

Question:	What is your birthplace?
Answer:	India.
Question:	What is your marital status?
Answer:	I am married.
Question:	What is your marital status?
Answer:	I am divorced.
Question:	Are you married?
Answer:	No, I am single.
Question:	Have you ever been married previously?
Answer:	Yes, I was married for one year when I lived in Mexico.
Question:	Is your husband a United States citizen?
Answer:	No, he is not a United States citizen.
Question:	Is your wife a United States citizen?
Answer:	Yes, she is.
Question:	Why did you get a divorce?
Answer:	We fought too much.
Question:	How long have you been married?
Answer:	I have been married for ten years.
Question:	How long have you been a Permanent Resident of the United States?
Answer:	I have been a resident for ten years.
Question:	When did you first come to the United States?
Answer:	I came to the United States in 1996.
Question:	On what date did you enter the United States?
Answer:	I entered the United States on September 5, 1996.
Question:	How long have you lived in the United States?
Answer:	I have lived in the United States for ten years.
Question:	What was your port of entry?
Answer:	My port of entry was JFK Airport in New York City.
Question:	Where did you enter the United States?
Answer:	I crossed the United States border near Seattle, Washington.
Question:	When did you become a Permanent Resident?
Answer:	I became a Permanent Resident in 1998.

Question:	In what year did you come to the United States?
Answer:	I came to the United States in 1996.
Question:	Who is your employer?
Answer:	I am unemployed right now.
Question:	Why aren't you working?
Answer:	I was laid off from my last job, and I'm looking for a new job.
Question:	Who is your current employer?
Answer:	My employer is Machines, Inc.
Question:	Whom do you currently work for?
Answer:	I work for Machines, Inc.
Question:	Are you currently working?
Answer:	Yes, I work for Machines, Inc.
Question:	What kind of work do you do?
Answer:	I work for Machines, Inc. as a factory worker.
Question:	Do you have a job?
Answer:	Yes, I work at Machines, Inc.
Question:	What is your occupation?
Answer:	I am a factory worker.
Question:	How do you support yourself?
Answer:	I work for Machines, Inc.
Question:	How long have you held this job?
Answer:	I have had this job for three years.
Question:	Who was your employer before that?
Answer:	I used to work for Southwest Airlines.
Question:	What job did you have there?
Answer:	I worked as a shipping clerk.
Question:	How many children do you have?
Answer:	I have three children.
Question:	Do your children live with you?
Answer:	Yes, my children live in my home.
Question:	How many people live in your house?
Answer:	Five people: myself, my husband, and three children.

Question:	Who do you live with?
Answer:	I live with my husband and three children.
Question:	Where do your children live?
Answer:	My children live with me in Brooklyn, New York.
Question:	Did any of your children stay in your native country?
Answer:	No, all of my children live with me here in Brooklyn.
Question:	When were your children born?
Answer:	One was born in 1992, one in 1994, and one in 1997.
Question:	Were they all born in the United States?
Answer:	Yes, they were born in America.
Question:	How many times have you left the United States since you became a Permanent Resident?
Answer:	I left the United States only one time.
Question:	How long were you away?
Answer:	I was gone for three weeks.
Question:	Where did you go?
Answer:	I went to visit my aunt in Poland.
Question:	Why did you leave the United States?
Answer:	I wanted to visit my aunt in Poland because she was dying.
Question:	Since becoming a Permanent Resident, have you ever left the United States?
Answer:	I left only once to go visit my grandmother in Mexico.
Question:	When was the last time you left the United States?
Answer:	I went to Canada two years ago.
Question:	Have you left the United States since you became a Permanent Resident?
Answer:	No, I've never left the United States.
Question:	Since coming to the United States, have you traveled to any other country?
Answer:	No, I've never left the United States.
Question:	Have you visited any other country since becoming a Permanent Resident?
Answer:	Yes, I went to Poland to visit my aunt one time.

Question:	Have you ever been deported by the immigration office?
Answer:	No, I have never been ordered to leave the United States.
Question:	Were you ever ordered to leave the United States?
Answer:	No, I have never been deported.
Question:	Have you ever used a different name?
Answer:	Yes, my last name used to be Martínez.
Question:	Do you want to change your name?
Answer:	Yes, I want to change my last name to Martin.
Question:	What other names have you gone by?
Answer:	I used to be called Pedro Martínez.
Question:	To what do you want to change your name?
Answer:	I want my new name to be Peter Martin.
Question:	What name do you want to have now?
Answer:	Peter Martin.
Question:	How do you spell that?
Answer:	P-e-t-e-r M-a-r-t-i-n.
Question:	What other names have you used in the past?
Answer:	I've never used any other names.
Question:	What was your maiden name?
Answer:	Before I was married, my name was Ana López.
Question:	What other names have you used in the past?
Answer:	Ana López.
Question:	When did you change your name?
Answer:	I changed my name ten years ago when I was married.
Question:	Why do you want to be an American citizen?
Answer:	I want to vote.
Question:	Why do you want to be a U.S. citizen?
Answer:	I want to travel with a U.S. passport.
Question:	Why have you applied for naturalization?
Answer:	I want to bring my mother to the United States.
Question:	Were you ever arrested?
Answer:	Yes, a long time ago.

Question:	What were you arrested for?
Answer:	I stole some money from the corner store.
Question:	How about any other arrests?
Answer:	No, that was the only time I was arrested.
Question:	Have you ever committed any crime for which you have not been arrested?
Answer:	No, I've never committed any crimes that I wasn't punished for.
Question:	Have you ever been imprisoned for breaking any law?
Answer:	I was in jail for three months for robbing the corner store.
Question:	When was that?
Answer:	During the winter of 1989.
Question:	Have you ever been a habitual drunkard?
Answer:	No, I don't drink alcohol.
Question:	Have you ever been a habitual drunkard?
Answer:	No, I drink only a little.
Question:	Have you ever advocated or practiced polygamy?
Answer:	No, I have only one wife.
Question:	Have you ever been married to more than one person at a time?
Answer:	No, I have always had only one husband.
Question:	Have you ever practiced polygamy?
Answer:	No, I am not married, and I have never been married.
Question:	Have you ever been a prostitute?
Answer:	No, I don't sell my body.
Question:	Have you ever been a prostitute?
Answer:	No, I've never taken money for sex.
Question:	Have you ever sold your body for money?
Answer:	No, I've never been a prostitute.
Question:	Have you ever knowingly and for gain helped any alien to enter the United States illegally?
Answer:	No, I have never smuggled anyone into the country.
Question:	Have you ever helped someone enter the United States illegally?
Answer:	No, I have never smuggled anyone into the country.

Question:	Have you ever smuggled anyone into the United States?
Answer:	No, I have never helped anyone enter the United States illegally.
Question:	Have you ever accepted money for sneaking someone into the United States?
Answer:	No, I have never helped anyone enter the United States illegally.
Question:	Have you ever been a trafficker in illegal drugs?
Answer:	No, I have never touched illegal drugs.
Question:	Have you ever bought or sold illegal drugs?
Answer:	No, I have never purchased or sold illegal drugs.
Question:	Have you ever carried illegal drugs for someone else?
Answer:	No, I have never handled illegal drugs.
Question:	Have you ever received income from illegal gambling?
Answer:	No, I don't gamble.
Question:	Did you ever get money illegally from gambling?
Answer:	No, I don't gamble for money.
Question:	Have you ever received money from illegal gambling?
Answer:	No, I don't gamble for money.
Question:	Have you ever received money or other goods from illegal gambling?
Answer:	No, I don't bet on anything.
Question:	Have you ever claimed in writing or in any other way to be a U.S. citizen?
Answer:	No, I have never lied about my citizenship.
Question:	Have you ever claimed in writing or in any other way to be a U.S. citizen?
Answer:	No, I never pretended to be a U.S. citizen.
Question:	Have you ever voted or registered to vote in the United States?
Answer:	No, I have never tried to vote because I am not a U.S. citizen.
Question:	Have you ever used a false name?
Answer:	No, I have never lied about my name.
Question:	Do you believe in the Constitution and the government of the United States?
Answer:	Yes, I support the Constitution and the government.

Question:	Do you believe in the government of the United States?
Answer:	Yes, I think the government is very good.
Question:	Are you willing to take the full Oath of Allegiance to the United States?
Answer:	Yes, I am ready to help my new country.
Question:	Are you willing to take the full Oath of Allegiance to the United States?
Answer:	Yes, I promise to help my new country.
Question:	Are you willing to take the full Oath of Allegiance to the United States?
Answer:	Yes, I want to do what is best for United States.
Question:	Have you ever been declared legally incompetent or confined as a patient in a mental institution?
Answer:	No, I am not crazy.
Question:	Were you ever in a mental hospital?
Answer:	No, I am mentally competent.
Question:	Have you ever been confined as a patient in a mental institution?
Answer:	No, I've never been in a mental hospital.
Question:	Were you born with or have you acquired any title of nobility?
Answer:	No, my parents were not royalty.
Question:	Are you a king, queen, duke, earl, or prince, or do you have any other title of nobility?
Answer:	No, I don't have any special titles along with my name and I am not a king or any other noble.
Question:	Were you born with or have you acquired any title of nobility?
Answer:	No, no one in my family is related to a king or queen.
Question:	Have you at any time ever ordered or otherwise participated in the persecution of any person because of race, religion, national origin, or political opinion?
Answer:	No, I don't hurt people because of what they believe or what color they are.
Question:	Have you ever participated in the persecution of any person because of race, religion, national origin, or political opinion?
Answer:	No, I have never persecuted anyone.

Question:	If the law requires it, are you willing to perform noncombatant services in the Armed Forces of the United States?
Answer:	Yes, I will help the soldiers when the law tells me.
Question:	Are you willing to perform noncombatant services in the Armed Forces of the United States if the law says you must?
Answer:	Yes, I will help the Armed Forces if the law tells me.
Question:	If the law requires it, are you willing to perform work of national importance under civilian direction?
Answer:	Yes, I will do anything to help the United States when the law says I must.
Question:	Will you perform work of national importance under civilian direction, when the law says you must?
Answer:	Yes, I will do anything to help the United States whenever it is needed.
Question:	Have you ever left the United States to avoid being drafted into the U.S. Armed Forces?
Answer:	No, I have never gone away to avoid going into the military.
Question:	Have you ever left the United States to avoid being drafted?
Answer:	No, I have never left the country so I didn't have to go to war.
Question:	Have you ever failed to comply with Selective Service laws?
Answer:	No, I never withheld my name for becoming a soldier.
Question:	Have you ever failed to comply with Selective Service laws?
Answer:	No, I have always given my name so I could be called to fight.
Question:	Did you register for the Selective Service?
Answer:	Yes, I gave my name to the government.
Question:	Do you know your Selective Service number?
Answer:	Yes, I have that number written on this paper.
Question:	Did you ever apply for exemption from military service because of alienage, conscientious objections, or other reasons?
Answer:	No, I have never said that I would not fight for the United States.
Question:	Have you ever tried to avoid military service?
Answer:	No, I have always been willing to be a soldier.
Question:	Did you ever request to stay out of the Armed Forces because of your religious beliefs?
Answer:	No, I have never been requested to serve in the armed forces.

Question:	Have you ever deserted from the military, air, or naval forces of the United States?
Answer:	No, I have never even been in the Armed Forces.
Question:	Have you ever deserted from the military, air, or naval forces of the United States?
Answer:	No, I was honorably discharged from the army.
Question:	Did you leave the Armed Forces before you were allowed to?
Answer:	No, I was in the Armed Forces for a full three years.
Question:	Are you a member of the Communist Party?
Answer:	No, I am not a member of any political group.
Question:	Have you ever been a member of the Communist Party?
Answer:	No, I never joined that group.
Question:	Are you now or have you ever been a member of the Communist Party?
Answer:	I am not a member now, but I was many years ago.
Question:	When was that?
Answer:	I joined in 1972, but I never went to the meetings.
Question:	Have you ever been affiliated with the Nazi Party?
Answer:	No, I don't agree with the Nazi Party.
Question:	Have you ever been a member of the Nazi Party?
Answer:	No, I never joined the Nazi Party.
Question:	Did you help the Nazi government in any way?
Answer:	No, I never assisted the Nazis.
Question:	Were you a part of the Nazi Party between 1933 and 1945?
Answer:	No, I was not.
Question:	Are you a member of any clubs or organizations?
Answer:	No, I am not a part of any organized groups.
Question:	Are you a member of any clubs or organizations?
Answer:	Yes, I am a member of the Small Business Association.
Question:	Have you ever given false testimony to obtain an immigration benefit?
Answer:	No, I have never lied before a judge.
Question:	Have you ever lied to obtain an immigration benefit?
Answer:	No, I have never given false testimony.

Question:	Have you ever lied at an immigration interview when you were under oath?
Answer:	No, I have never lied after swearing to tell the truth.
Question:	If the law requires it, are you willing to bear arms on behalf of the United States?
Answer:	Yes, I will fight in a war to help the United States.
Question:	If the law requires it, are you willing to bear arms on behalf of the United States?
Answer:	Yes, I will be a soldier if the law tells me.
Question:	Are you willing to bear arms for the United States, even if it is against the country you used to live in?
Answer:	Yes, I will fight for the United States, even if it is against my old country.

CAPÍTULO 8

Ejemplos de oraciones de dictado

✪ Examples of Oral Dictation / Ejemplos de oraciones de dictado

It is important to practice sentence dictation in English. Ask a friend or family member to read these sentences out loud. Try to write the sentences without looking at the page.

Es importante practicar el dictado de oraciones en inglés. Pide que un amigo o un familiar lea las oraciones en voz alta. Trata de escribirlas sin mirarlas.

1. I want to be an American citizen.

2. I am studying English.

3. I live in the United States.

4. I like living in the United States.

5. I live with my family.

6. I have a wife and two children.

7. I work at a factory.

8. I work five days a week.

9. My children go to school.

10. My wife has a job too.

11. We plan to live in the United States forever.

12. The weather is nice today.

13. It is very sunny.

14. I enjoy warm weather.

15. My wife and I like to cook.

16. My children help us cook.

17. We eat lots of food at dinner.

18. I have a car.

19. My car is blue.

20. Sometimes I ride the bus.

21. I work in the city.

22. I have a dog.

23. My dog is big and brown.

24. I have a big brown dog.

25. I like to play with my dog.

26. Today is Tuesday.

27. Yesterday was Monday.

28. Tomorrow is Wednesday.

29. Next week I have a vacation from my work.

30. It is hot in the summer.

31. It is cold in the winter.

32. I love my family.

33. My wife and I work hard.

34. The boy is running.

35. The boy runs very fast.

36. The girl is wearing a dress.

37. The girl's dress is pretty.

38. The girl is wearing a very pretty dress.

39. Today I need to vote for mayor.

40. Today I need to vote for president.

41. Today I need to vote for mayor and president.

42. It is my right to vote.

43. Every citizen should vote.

44. My family and I live in a house.

45. Our apartment is nice.

46. We used to live in a different city.

47. We like living in this city.

48. I like to listen to music.

49. I like to read the newspaper.

50. The children like to play games.

1. _____

2. _____

3. _____

4. _____

5. _____

6. _____

7. _____

8. _____

9. _____

10. _____

11. _____

12. _____

13. _____

14. _____

15. _____

16. _____

17. _____

18. _____

19. _____

20. _____

21. _____

22. _____

23. _____

24. _____

25. _____

26. _____

27. _____

28. _____

29. _____

30. _____

31. _____

32. _____

33. _____

34. _____

35. _____

36. _____

37. _____

38. _____

39. _____

40. _____

41. _____

42. _____

43. _____

44. _____

45. _____

46. _____

47. _____

48. _____

49. _____

50. _____

APÉNDICE A

✪ Información de contacto

Como ponerse en contacto con el USCIS

Teléfono: **1-800-375-5283**
TTY: **1-800-767-1833**
Sitio web: **www.uscis.gov**

Oficinas del USCIS por Estado

ALABAMA
Atlanta, Georgia District Office
Martin Luther King Jr. Federal Building
77 Forsyth Street, SW
Atlanta, GA 30303

ALASKA
Anchorage
620 East 10th Avenue
Suite 10
Anchorage, AL 99501

ARIZONA
Phoenix
2035 North Central Avenue
Phoenix, AZ 85004

Tucson
6431 South Country Club Road
Tucson, AZ 85706-5907
(Suboffice serving Cochise, Pima, Santa Cruz, Graham, and Pinal.)

ARKANSAS
Fort Smith
4977 Old Greenwood Road
Fort Smith, AR 72903
(Suboffice serving western Arkansas. The district office is located in New Orleans.)

CALIFORNIA
Los Angeles
300 North Los Angeles Street
Room 1001
Los Angeles, CA 90012
(District office serving Los Angeles, Orange, Riverside, San Bernardino, Santa Barbara, San Luis Obispo, and Ventura counties. There are also offices in East Los Angeles, El Monte, Bell, Bellflower, Westminster, Santa Ana, Camarillo, Riverside, San Pedro, Los Angeles International Airport, Lompoc, and Lancaster.)

San Bernardino
655 West Rialto Avenue
San Bernardino, CA 92410-3327

San Diego
880 Front Street
Suite 1234
San Diego, CA 92101
(District office serving San Diego and Imperial counties.)

San Francisco

444 Washington Street

San Francisco, CA 94111

(District office serving Alameda, Contra Costa, Del Norte, Humboldt, Lake, Marin, Mendocino, Napa, San Francisco, San Mateo, Sonoma, and Trinity.)

Fresno

1177 Fulton Mall

Fresno, CA 93721-1913

(Suboffice serving Fresno, Inyo, Kern, Kings, Madera, Mariposa, Merced, Mono, and Tulare.)

Sacramento

650 Capitol Mall

Sacramento, CA 95814

(Suboffice serving Alpine, Amador, Butte, Calaveras, Colusa, El Dorado, Glenn, Lassen, Modoc, Nevada, Placer, Plumas, Sacramento, San Joaquin, Shasta, Sierra, Sutter, Siskiyou, Solano, Tehama, Tuolumne, Yolo, and Yuba.)

San Jose

1887 Monterey Road

San Jose, CA 95112

(Suboffice serving Monterey, San Benito, Santa Clara, and Santa Cruz.)

Santa Ana

34 Civic Center Plaza

Federal Building

Santa Ana, CA 92701

COLORADO

Denver

4730 Paris Street

Denver, CO 80239

CONNECTICUT

Hartford

450 Main Street

4th Floor

Hartford, CT 06103-3060

(Suboffice serving Connecticut. The district office is located in Boston.)

DELAWARE

Dover

1305 McD Drive

Dover, DE 19901

(Satellite office. District office is in Philadelphia.)

DISTRICT OF COLUMBIA (WASHINGTON, D.C.)

2675 Propensity Avenue

Fairfax, VA 22031

(District office serving the entire state of Virginia and the District of Columbia)

FLORIDA

Miami

7880 Biscayne Boulevard

Miami, FL 33138

(District office)

Jacksonville

4121 Southpoint Boulevard

Jacksonville, FL 32216

(Suboffice serving Alachua, Baker, Bay, Bradford, Calhoun, Clay, Columbia, Dixie, Duval, Escambia, Franklin, Gadsden, Gilchrist, Gulf, Hamilton, Holmes, Jackson, Jefferson, Lafayette, Leon, Levy, Liberty, Madison, Nassau, Okaloosa, Putnum, Santa Rosa, St. Johns, Suwanee, Taylor, Union, Wakulla, Walton, and Washington.)

Orlando

9403 Tradeport Drive

Orlando, FL 32827

(Suboffice serving Orange, Osceola, Seminole, Lake, Brevard, Flagler, Volusia, Marion, and Sumter.)

Tampa

5524 West Cypress Street

Tampa, FL 33607-1708

(Suboffice serving Citrus, Hernando, Pasco, Pinellas, Hillsborough, Polk, Hardee, Manatee, Sarasota, De Soto, Charlotte, and Lee.)

West Palm Beach

326 Fern Street,

Suite 200

West Palm Beach, FL 33401

(Suboffice serving Palm Beach, Martin, St. Lucie, Indian River, Okeechobee, Hendry, Glades, and Highland counties.)

GEORGIA

Atlanta

Martin Luther King, Jr. Federal Building

77 Forsyth Street, SW

Atlanta, GA 30303

GUAM

Agana

Sirena Plaza

108 Hernan Cortez Avenue

Suite 100

Hagatna, Guam 96910

(Suboffice serving Guam and the Northern Mariana
Islands. District office is located in Honolulu.)

HAWAII

Honolulu

595 Ala Moana Boulevard

Honolulu, HI 96813

(District office serving Hawaii, the Territory of Guam, and
the Commonwealth of Northern Marianas.)

IDAHO

Boise

1185 South Vinnell Way

Room 108

Boise, ID 83709

(Suboffice serving southwest and south central Idaho. The
district office is located in Helena, Montana.)

ILLINOIS

Chicago

101 West Congress Parkway

Chicago, IL 60605

INDIANA

Indianapolis

Indianapolis, IN 46204-3915

(Suboffice serving the state of Indiana except Lake, Porter,
LaPorte, and St. Joseph counties in northwest Indiana.
Residents of those four counties are served by the
Chicago district office.)

IOWA

Des Moines

210 Walnut Street

Room 369

Federal Building

Des Moines, IA 50309

(Satellite office. The district office is located in Omaha,
Nebraska.)

KANSAS

Wichita

271 West 3rd Street North

Suite 1050

Wichita, KS 67202-1212

(Satellite office serving western Kansas. The district office
is located in Kansas City, Missouri.)

KENTUCKY

Louisville

USCIS–Louisville

Room 390

601 West Broadway

Louisville, KY 40202

(Suboffice serving Kentucky.)

LOUISIANA

New Orleans

Metairie Centre

2424 Edenbom Avenue

Third Floor (Suite 300)

Metairie, LA 70001

(Serving Louisiana, Arkansas, Tennessee, and Kentucky.)

MAINE

Portland

176 Gannett Drive

South Portland, ME 04106

(Serving Maine and Vermont.)

MARYLAND

Baltimore

Fallon Federal Building

31 Hopkins Plaza

Baltimore, MD 21201

MASSACHUSETTS

Boston

John F. Kennedy Federal Building

Government Center

Boston, MA 02203

MICHIGAN

Detroit

333 Mt. Elliott

Detroit, MI 48207

MINNESOTA

St. Paul

2901 Metro Drive

Suite 100

Bloomington, MN 55425

(Serving Minnesota, North Dakota, and South Dakota.)

MISSISSIPPI

New Orleans District Office (see Louisiana)

MISSOURI

Kansas City
9747 Northwest Conant Avenue
Kansas City, MO 64153
(District office serving Missouri and Kansas.)

St. Louis
Robert A. Young Federal Building
1222 Spruce Street
Room 1.100
St. Louis, Missouri 63103-2815
(Suboffice serving eastern part of Missouri.)

MONTANA

Helena
2800 Skyway Drive
Helena, MT 59602
(District office for Montana and portions of Idaho.)

NEBRASKA

Omaha
1717 Avenue H
Omaha, NE 68110-2752
(District office serving Nebraska and Iowa.)

NEVADA

Las Vegas
3373 Pepper Lane
Las Vegas, NV 89120-2739
(Suboffice serving Clark, Esmeralda, Nye, and Lincoln counties. The district office is located in Phoenix, AZ.)

Reno
1351 Corporate Boulevard
Reno, NV 89502
(Suboffice servicing Carson, Churchill, Douglas, Elko, Eureka, Humboldt, Lander, Lyon, Mineral, Pershing, Storey, Washoe, and White Pine counties.)

NEW HAMPSHIRE

Manchester
803 Canal Street
Manchester, NH 03101

NEW JERSEY

Newark
970 Broad Street
Newark, NJ 07102
(District office serving Bergen, Essex, Hudson, Hunterdon, Middlesex, Morris, Passaic, Somerset, Sussex, Union, and Warren counties.)

Cherry Hill
1886 Greentree Road
Cherry Hill, NJ 08003
(Suboffice serving Atlantic, Burlington, Camden, Cape May, Cumberland, Gloucester, Mercer, Monmouth, Ocean, and Salem counties.)

NEW MEXICO

Albuquerque
1720 Randolph Road, SE
Albuquerque, NM 87106
(Suboffice serving northern New Mexico. The district office is located in El Paso, Texas.)

NEW YORK

Buffalo
Federal Center
130 Delaware Avenue
Buffalo, NY 14202
(District office serving the state of New York, with the exception of New York City and its surrounding counties.)

New York City
26 Federal Plaza
New York, NY 10278
(District office serving the five boroughs of New York City, Nassau, Suffolk, Dutchess, Orange, Putnam, Rockland, Sullivan, Ulster, and Westchester counties.)

Albany
1086 Troy-Schenectady Road
Latham, New York 12110
(Suboffice serving Albany, Broome, Chenango, Clinton, Columbia, Delaware, Essex, Franklin, Fulton, Greene, Hamilton, Herkimer, Madison, Montgomery, Oneida, Otsego, Rensselaer, Saint Lawrence, Saratoga, Schenectady, Schoharie, Tioga, Warren, and Washington.)

NORTH CAROLINA

Charlotte
6130 Tyvola Centre Drive
Charlotte, NC 28217
(Suboffice serving North Carolina. The district office is located in Atlanta.)

NORTH DAKOTA

St. Paul, Minnesota District Office
2901 Metro Drive
Suite 100
Bloomington, MN 55425

OHIO

Cleveland
AJC Federal Building
1240 East Ninth Street
Room 501
Cleveland, OH 44199
(District office serving the northern part of Ohio.)

Cincinnati
J.W. Peck Federal Building
550 Main Street
Room 4001
Cincinnati, OH 45202
(Suboffice serving the southern part of Ohio.)

Columbus
Leveque Tower
50 West Broad Street
Suite 306
Columbus, OH 43215

OKLAHOMA

Oklahoma City
4400 SW 44th Street
Suite "A"
Oklahoma City, OK 73119-2800
(Suboffice serving Oklahoma. District office is located in Dallas.)

OREGON

Portland
511 NW Broadway
Portland, OR 97209
(District office serving Oregon.)

PENNSYLVANIA

Philadelphia
1600 Callowhill Street
Philadelphia, PA 19130
(District office for Pennsylvania, Delaware, and West Virginia.)

Pittsburgh
300 Sidney Street
Pittsburgh, PA 15203
(Suboffice serving western Pennsylvania and West Virginia.)

PUERTO RICO

San Juan
San Patricio Office Center
7 Tabonuco Street
Suite 100
Guaynabo, PR 00968
(District office serving Puerto Rico and the U.S. Virgin Islands.)

RHODE ISLAND

Providence
200 Dyer Street
Providence, RI 02903
(Suboffice serving Rhode Island. The district office is located in Boston.)

SOUTH CAROLINA

Charleston
1 Poston Road
Suite 130
Parkshore Center
Charleston, SC 29407
(Suboffice serving South Carolina. The district office is located in Atlanta.)

SOUTH DAKOTA

St. Paul, Minnesota District Office
2901 Metro Drive
Suite 100
Bloomington, MN 55425

TENNESSEE*

Memphis
842 Virginia Pen Cove
Memphis, TN 38122
(Suboffice serving the eastern half of Arkansas, the northern half of Mississippi, and the state of Tennessee. The district office is located in New Orleans.)
*(Naturalization cases in Anderson, Bedford, Bledsoe, Blount, Bradley, Campbell, Carter, Claiborne, Cocke, Coffee, Franklin, Grainger, Greene, Grundy, Hamblen, Hamilton, Hancock, Hawkins, Jefferson, Johnson, Knox, Lincoln, Loudon, Marion, McMinn, Meigs, Monroe, Moore, Morgan, Polk, Rhea, Roane, Scott, Sequatchie, Sevier, Sullivan, Unicoi, Union, Van Buren, Warren, and Washington counties fall under the jurisdiction of the Louisville, Kentucky suboffice.)

TEXAS

Dallas
8101 North Stemmons Freeway
Dallas, TX 75247
(District office serving 123 northern counties in the state of Texas and all of Oklahoma.)

El Paso
1545 Hawkins Boulevard
Suite 167
El Paso, TX 79925
(District office serving West Texas and New Mexico.)

Harlingen
1717 Zoy Street
Harlingen, TX 78552
(District office serving Brooks, Cameron, Hidalgo, Kennedy,
   Kleberg, Starr, and Willacy.)

Houston
126 Northpoint
Houston, TX 77060
(District office serving southeastern Texas.)

San Antonio
8940 Fourwinds Drive
San Antonio, TX 78239
(District office serving central and south Texas.)

UTAH
Salt Lake City
5272 South College Drive, #100
Murray, UT 84123
(Suboffice serving Utah. The district office is located in Denver.)

VERMONT
St. Albans
64 Gricebrook Road
St. Albans, VT 05478
(Suboffice serving Vermont and New Hampshire. The
   district office is located in Portland, Maine.)

U.S. VIRGIN ISLANDS
Charlotte Amalie
8000 Nisky Center
Suite 1A First Floor South
Charlotte Amalie,
St. Thomas, USVI 00802
(Suboffice serving St. Thomas and St. John. The district
   office is located in San Juan.)

St. Croix
Sunny Isle Shopping Center
Christiansted
St. Croix, USVI 00823
(Suboffice serving St. Croix, U.S. Virgin Islands. The district
   office is located in San Juan.)

VIRGINIA
Norfolk
5280 Henneman Drive
Norfolk, Virginia 23513
(Suboffice serving southeastern Virginia. The district office
   is located in Washington, D.C.)

WASHINGTON
Seattle
12500 Tukwila International Boulevard
Seattle WA 98168
(District office serving Washington, and ten northern
   counties in Idaho.)

Spokane
U.S. Courthouse
920 West Riverside
Room 691
Spokane, WA 99201
(Suboffice serving Adams, Benton, Chelan, Asotin,
   Columbia, Douglas, Ferry, Garfield, Grant, Lincoln,
   Okanogan, Pend O'reille, Spokane, Stevens, Walla
   Walla, and Whitman.)

Yakima
415 North Third Street
Yakima, WA 98901
(Suboffice serving Kittitas, Klickitat, and Yakima.)

WISCONSIN
Milwaukee
310 East Knapp Street
Milwaukee, WI 53202
(Suboffice serving Wisconsin. The district office is located in
   Chicago.)

International Embassies in the United States

The Republic of Afghanistan
2341 Wyoming Avenue NW
Washington, D.C. 20008
Tel: 202-483-6410
Fax: 202-483-6488
www.embassyofafghanistan.org

The Republic of Albania
2100 S Street NW
Washington, D.C. 20008
Tel: 202-223-4942
Fax: 202-628-7342
www.albaniaembassy.org

The Democratic and Popular Republic of Algeria
2118 Kalorama Road NW
Washington, D.C. 20008
Tel: 202-265-2800
Fax: 202-667-2174
www.algeria-us.org

The Embassy of The Republic of Angola
1615 M Street NW
Suite 900
Washington, D.C. 20036
Tel: 202-785-1156
Fax: 202-785-1258

Embassy of Antigua and Barbuda
3216 New Mexico Avenue NW
Washington, D.C. 20016
Tel: 202-362-5122
Fax: 202-362-5225

The Argentine Republic
1600 New Hampshire Avenue NW
Washington, D.C. 20009
Tel: 202-238-6400
Fax: 202-332-3171
www.embassyofargentina.us

Embassy of the Republic of Armenia
2225 R Street
Washington, D.C. 20008
Tel: 202-319-1976
Fax: 202-319-2982
www.armeniaemb.org

Embassy of Australia
1601 Massachusetts Avenue NW
Washington, D.C. 20036
Tel: 202-797-3000
Fax: 202-797-3168
www.austemb.org

Austrian Press & Information Service
3524 International Court NW
Washington, D.C. 20008-3035
Tel: 202-895-6700
Fax: 202-895-6750
www.austria.org

The Republic of Azerbaijan
927 15th Street NW
Suite 700
Washington, D.C. 20035
Tel: 202-337-3500
Fax: 202-337-5911
www.azembassy.us

The Commonwealth of the Bahamas
2220 Massachusetts Avenue NW
Washington, D.C. 20008
Tel: 202-319-2660
Fax: 202-319-2668

Embassy of the State of Bahrain
3502 International Drive NW
Washington, D.C. 20008
Tel: 202-342-0741
Fax: 202-362-2192
www.bahrainembassy.org

The People's Republic of Bangladesh
3510 International Drive NW
Washington, D.C. 20008
Tel: 202-244-2745
Fax: 202-244-5366
www.bangladoot.org

Barbados
2144 Wyoming Avenue NW
Washington, D.C. 20008
Tel: 202-939-9200
Fax: 202-332-7467

Embassy of the Republic of Belarus
1619 New Hampshire Avenue NW
Washington, D.C. 20009
Tel: 202-986-1606
Fax: 202-986-1805
www.belarusembassy.org

Embassy of Belgium
3330 Garfield Street NW
Washington, D.C. 20008
Tel: 202-333-6900
Fax: 202-333-3079
www.diplobel.us

Belize
2535 Massachusetts Avenue NW
Washington, D.C. 20008
Tel: 202-332-9636
Fax: 202-332-6888
www.embassyofbelize.org

Embassy of the Republic of Benin
2124 Kalorama Road NW
Washington, D.C. 20008
Tel: 202-232-6656
Fax: 202-265-1996

Bolivia
3014 Massachusetts Avenue NW
Washington, D.C. 20008
Tel: 202-483-4410
Fax: 202-328-3712
www.bolivia-usa.org

Embassy of Bosnia and Herzegovina
2109 E Street NW
Washington, D.C. 20037
Tel: 202-337-1500
Fax: 202-337-1502
www.bosnianembassy.org

Botswana
1531-3 New Hampshire Avenue NW
Washington, D.C. 20036
Tel: 202-244-4990
Fax: 202-244-4164
www.botswanaembassy.org

Brazil
3006 Massachusetts Avenue NW
Washington, D.C. 20008
Tel: 202-238-2700
Fax: 202-238-2827
www.brasilemb.org

Embassy of Brunei Darussalam
3520 International Court NW
Washington, D.C. 20008
Tel: 202-237-1838
Fax: 202-885-0560
www.bruneiembassy.org

Embassy of Burkina Faso
2340 Massachusetts Avenue NW
Washington, D.C. 20008
Tel: 202-332-5577
Fax: 202-667-1882
www.burkinaembassy-usa.org

The Republic of Bulgaria
1621 22nd Street NW
Washington, D.C. 20008
Tel: 202-387-0174
Fax: 202-234-7973
www.bulgaria-embassy.org

Embassy of the Republic of Burundi
2233 Wisconsin Avenue NW
Suite 212
Washington, D.C. 20007
Tel: 202-342-2574
Fax: 202-342-2578
www.burundiembassy-usa.org

Embassy of the Republic of Cameroon
2349 Massachusetts Avenue NW
Washington, D.C. 20008
Tel: 202-265-8790
Fax: 202-387-3826

Royal Embassy of Camodia
4500 16th Street NW
Washington, D.C. 20011
Tel: 202-726-7742
Fax: 202-726-8381
www.embassyofcambodia.org

Canada
501 Pennsylvania Avenue NW
Washington, D.C. 20001
Tel: 202-682-1740
Fax: 202-682-7726
www.canadianembassy.org

The Republic of Cape Verde
3415 Massachusetts Avenue NW
Washington, D.C. 20007
Tel: 202-965-6820
Fax: 202-965-1207
www.capeverdeusa.org

The Central African Republic
1618 22nd Street NW
Washington, D.C. 20008
Tel: 202-483-7800
Fax: 202-332-9893

The Republic of Chad
2002 R Street NW
Washington, D.C. 20009
Tel: 202-462-4009
Fax: 202-265-1937
www.chadembassy.org

Chile
1732 Massachusetts Avenue NW
Washington, D.C. 20036
Tel: 202-785-1746
Fax: 202-887-5579
www.chile-usa.org

Embassy of the People's Republic of China
2300 Connecticut Avenue NW
Washington, D.C. 20008
Tel: 202-328-2500
Fax: 202-588-0032
www.china-embassy.org

The Embassy of Columbia
2118 Leroy Place NW
Washington, D.C. 20008
Tel: 202-387-8338
Fax: 202-232-8643
www.colombiaemb.net

The Republic of Congo
4891 Colorado Avenue NW
Washington, D.C. 20011
Tel: 202-726-5500
Fax: 202-726-1860
www.embassyofcongo.org

Embassy of the Democratic Republic of Congo
1800 New Hampshire Avenue NW
Washington, D.C. 20009
Tel: 202-234-7690
Fax: 202-234-2609

Embassy of Costa Rica
2114 S Street NW
Washington, D.C. 20008
Tel: 202-234-2945
Fax: 202-265-4795
www.costarica-embassy.org

The Republic of Côte d'Ivoire (Ivory Coast)
2424 Massachusetts Avenue NW
Washington, D.C. 20008
Tel: 202-797-0300

The Embassy of the Republic of Croatia
2343 Massachusetts Avenue NW
Washington, D.C. 20008
Tel: 202-588-5899
Fax: 202-588-8936
www.croatiaemb.org

Cuba Interests Section
2630 and 2639 16th Street NW
Washington, D.C. 20009
Tel: 202-797-8518
Fax: 202-986-7283

The Republic of Cyprus
2211 R Street NW
Washington, D.C. 20008
Tel: 202-462-5772
Fax: 202-483-6710
www.cyprusembassy.net

Embassy of the Czech Republic
3900 Spring of Freedom Street NW
Washington, D.C. 20008
Tel: 202-274-9100
Fax: 202-966-8540
www.mzv.cz/washington

Royal Danish Embassy
3200 Whitehaven Street NW
Washington, D.C. 20008
Tel: 202-234-4300
Fax: 202-328-1470
www.denmarkemb.org

Embassy of the Republic of Djibouti
1156 15th Street NW
Suite 515
Washington, D.C. 20005
Tel: 202-331-0270
Fax: 202-331-0302

The Commonwealth of Dominica
3216 New Mexico Avenue NW
Washington, D.C. 20016
Tel: 202-364-6781
Fax: 202-364-6791

Dominican Republic
1715 22nd Street NW
Washington, D.C. 20008
Tel: 202-332-6280
Fax: 202-265-8057
www.domrep.org

Embassy of East Timor
4201 Connecticut Avenue NW
Suite 504
Washington, D.C. 20008
Tel: 202-966-3202
Fax: 202-966-3205

The Embassy of Ecuador
2535 15th Street NW
Washington, D.C. 20009
Tel: 202-234-7200
Fax: 202-667-3482

The Arab Republic of Egypt
3521 International Court NW
Washington, D.C. 20008
Tel: 202-895-5400
Fax: 202-244-4319
www.egyptembassy.us

El Salvador
2308 California Street NW
Washington, D.C. 20008
Tel: 202-265-9671
www.elsalvador.org

Equatorial Guinea
2020 16th Street NW
Washington, D.C. 20009
Tel: 202-518-5700
Fax: 202-518-5252

Embassy of Eritrea
1708 New Hampshire Avenue NW
Washington, D.C. 20009
Tel: 202-319-1991
Fax: 202-319-1304

Embassy of Estonia
1730 M Street NW
Suite 503
Washington, D.C. 20036
Tel: 202-588-0101
Fax: 202-588-0108
www.estemb.org

Embassy of Ethiopia
3506 International Drive NW
Washington, D.C. 20008
Tel: 202-364-1200
Fax: 202-686-9551
www.ethiopianembassy.org

Embassy of Fiji
2233 Wisconsin Avenue NW
Suite 240
Washington, D.C. 20007
Tel: 202-337-8320
Fax: 202-337-1996

Embassy of Finland
3301 Massachusetts Avenue NW
Washington, D.C. 20008
Tel: 202-298-5800
Fax: 202-298-6030
www.finland.org

Embassy of France
4101 Reservoir Road NW
Washington, D.C. 20007
Tel: 202-944-6000
Fax: 202-944-6072
www.info-france-usa.org

Embassy of the Gabonese Republic
2034 20th Street NW
Suite 200
Washington, D.C. 20009
Tel: 202-797-1000
Fax: 202-332-0668

Embassy of the Gambia
1155 15th Street NW
Suite 1000
Washington, D.C. 20005
Tel: 202-785-1399
Fax: 202-785-1430
www.gambia.com/index.html

The Embassy of the Republic of Georgia
1615 New Hampshire Avenue NW
Suite 300
Washington, D.C. 20009
Tel: 202-387-2390
Fax: 202-393-4537
www.georgiaemb.org

German Embassy
4645 Reservoir Road
Washington, D.C. 20007-1998
Tel: 202-298-4000
Fax: 202-298-4249 or 202-333-2653
www.germany-info.org

Ghana
3512 International Drive NW
Washington, D.C. 20008
Tel: 202-686-4520
Fax: 202-686-4527
www.ghana-embassy.org

Embassy of Greece
2221 Massachusetts Avenue NW
Washington D.C. 20008
Tel: 202-939-1300
Fax: 202-939-1324
www.greekembassy.org

Grenada
1701 New Hampshire Avenue NW
Washington, D.C. 20009
Tel: 202-265-2561
Fax: 202-265-2468
www.grenadaembassyusa.org

Guatemala
2220 R Street NW
Washington, D.C. 20008
Tel: 202-745-4952
Fax: 202-745-1908
www.guatemala-embassy.org

The Republic of Guinea
2112 Leroy Place NW
Washington, D.C. 20008
Tel: 202-986-4300

Guyana
2490 Tracy Place NW
Washington, D.C. 20008
Tel: 202-265-6900
Fax: 202-232-1297

The Republic of Haiti
2311 Massachusetts Avenue NW
Washington, D.C. 20008
Tel: 202-332-4090
Fax: 202-745-7215
www.haiti.org

The Holy See (Apostolic Nunciature)
3339 Massachusetts Avenue NW
Washington, D.C. 20008
Tel: 202-333-7121

Honduras
3007 Tilden Street NW
Suite 4M
Washington, D.C. 20008
Tel: 202-966-7702
Fax: 202-966-9751
www.hondurasemb.org

The Embassy of the Republic of Hungary
3910 Shoemaker Street NW
Washington, D.C. 20008
Tel: 202-362-6730
Fax: 202-966-8135
www.huembwas.org

Embassy of Iceland
1156 15th Street NW
Suite 1200
Washington, D.C. 20005-1704
Tel: 202-265-6653
Fax: 202-265-6656
www.iceland.org

Embassy of India
2107 Massachusetts Avenue NW
Washington, D.C. 20008
Tel: 202-939-7000
Fax: 202-265-4351
www.indianembassy.org

The Republic of Indonesia
2020 Massachusetts Avenue NW
Washington, D.C. 20036
Tel: 202-775-5200
Fax: 202-775-5365
wwwembassyofindonesia.org

Iranian Interests Section
2209 Wisconsin Avenue NW
Washington, D.C. 20007
Tel: 202-965-4990
Fax: 202-965-1073
www.daftar.org/Eng/default.asp?lang=eng

Embassy of Iraq
1801 P Street NW
Washington, D.C. 20036
Tel: 202-483-7500
Fax: 202-462-5066
www.iraqembassy.org

Ireland
2234 Massachusetts Avenue NW
Washington, D.C. 20008
Tel: 202-462-3939
Fax: 202-232-5993
www.irelandemb.org

Embassy of Israel
3514 International Drive NW
Washington, D.C. 20008
Tel: 202-364-5500
Fax: 202-364-5428
www.israelemb.org

Embassy of Italy
3000 Whitehaven Street NW
Washington, D.C. 20008
Tel: 202-612-4400
Fax: 202-518-2154
www.italyemb.org

Jamaica
1520 New Hampshire Avenue NW
Washington, D.C. 20036
Tel: 202-452-0660
Fax: 202-452-0081
www.emjamusa.org

The Embassy of Japan
2520 Massachusetts Avenue NW
Washington, D.C. 20008
Tel: 202-238-6700
Fax: 202-328-2187
www.embjapan.org

Embassy of the Hashemite Kingdom of Jordan
3504 International Drive NW
Washington, D.C. 20008
Tel: 202-966-2664
Fax: 202-966-3110
www.jordanembassyus.org

The Republic of Kazakhstan
1401 16th Street NW
Washington, D.C. 20036
Tel: 202-232-5488
Fax: 202-232-5845
www.kazakhembus.org

Embassy of Kenya
2249 R Street NW
Washington, D.C. 20008
Tel: 202-387-6101
Fax: 202-462-3829
www.kenyaembassy.com

The Republic of Korea
2450 Massachusetts Avenue NW
Washington, D.C. 20008
Tel: 202-939-5600
Fax: 202-797-0595
www.koreaembassyusa.org

The State of Kuwait
2940 Tilden Street NW
Washington, D.C. 20008
Tel: 202-966-0702
Fax: 202-364-2868

The Kyrgyz Republic
2360 Massachusetts Avenue NW
Washington, D.C. 20007
Tel: 202-338-5141
Fax: 202-395-7550
www.kgembassy.org

The Lao People's Democratic Republic
2222 S Street NW
Washington, D.C. 20008
Tel: 202-332-6416
Fax: 202-332-4923
www.laoembassy.com

Latvia
4325 17th Street NW
Washington, D.C. 20011
Tel: 202-726-8213
Fax: 202-726-6785
www.latvia-usa.org

Lebanon
2560 28th Street NW
Washington, D.C. 20008
Tel: 202-939-6300
Fax: 202-939-6324
www.lebanonembassyus.org

Embassy of Lesotho
2511 Massachusetts Avenue NW
Washington, D.C. 20008
Tel: 202-797-5533
Fax: 202-234-6815

The Republic of Liberia
5201 16th Street NW
Washington, D.C. 20011
Tel: 202-723-0437
Fax: 202-723-0436
www.embassyofliberia.org

Embassy of Liechtenstein
888 17th Street NW
Suite 1250
Washington, D.C. 20006
Tel: 202-331-0590
Fax: 202-331-3221
http://www.liechtenstein.li/en/fl-aussenstelle-washington-
   home

The Embassy of Lithuania
2622 16th Street NW
Washington, D.C. 20009-4202
Tel: 202-234-5860
Fax: 202-328-0466
www.ltembassyus.org

Luxembourg
2200 Massachusetts Avenue NW
Washington, D.C. 20008
Tel: 202-265-4171
Fax: 202-328-8270

Embassy of the Republic of Macedonia
1101 30th Street NW
Suite 302
Washington, D.C. 20007
Tel: 202-337-3063
Fax: 202-337-3093
www.macedonianembassy.org

Embassy of Madagascar
2374 Massachusetts Avenue NW
Washington, D.C. 20008
Tel: 202-265-5525
www.embassy.org/madagascar

Embassy of Malawi
2408 Massachusetts Avenue NW
Washington, D.C. 20008
Tel: 202-797-1007

Malaysia
3516 International Court NW
Washington, D.C. 20008
Tel: 202-572-9700
Fax: 202-483-7661

The Republic of Mali
2130 R Street NW
Washington, D.C. 20008
Tel: 202-332-2249
Fax: 202-332-6603
www.maliembassy-usa.org

Malta
2017 Connecticut Avenue NW
Washington, D.C. 20008
Tel: 202-462-3611
Fax: 202-387-5470
http://malta.usembassy.gov

Embassy of the Republic of the Marshall Islands
2433 Massachusetts Avenue NW
Washington, D.C. 20008
Tel: 202-234-5414
Fax: 202-232-3236
www.rmiembassyus.org

The Islamic Republic of Mauritania
2129 Leroy Place NW
Washington, D.C. 20008
Tel: 202-232-5700
Fax: 202-319-2623
http://mauritania-usa.org

Mexico
1911 Pennsylvania Avenue NW
Washington, D.C. 20006
Tel: 202-728-1600
Fax: 202-728-1698
www.embassyofmexico.org

The Federated States of Micronesia
1725 N Street NW
Washington, D.C. 20036
Tel: 202-223-4383
Fax: 202-223-4391

The Republic of Moldova
2101 S Street NW
Washington, D.C. 20008
Tel: 202-667-1130/31/37
Fax: 202-667-1204
www.embassyrm.org

Mongolia
2833 M Street NW
Washington, D.C. 20007
Tel: 202-333-7117
Fax: 202-298-9227
www.mongolianembassy.com

The Kingdom of Morocco
1601 21st Street NW
Washington, D.C. 20009
Tel: 202-462-7979
Fax: 202-265-0161

The Republic of Mozambique
1990 M Street NW
Suite 570
Washington, D.C. 20036
Tel: 202-293-7146
Fax: 202-835-0245
www.embamoc-usa.org

Embassy of the Union of Myanmar
2300 S Street NW
Washington, D.C. 20008
Tel: 202-332-9044
Fax: 202-332-9046
www.mewashingtondc.com

Embassy of the Republic of Namibia
1605 New Hampshire Avenue NW
Washington, D.C. 20009
Tel: 202-986-0540
Fax: 202-986-0443
www.namibianembassyusa.org

Royal Nepalese Embassy
2131 Leroy Place NW
Washington, D.C. 20008
Tel: 202-667-4550
Fax: 202-667-5534

Royal Netherlands Embassy
4200 Linnean Avenue NW
Washington, D.C. 20008
Tel: 202-244-5300
Fax: 202-362-3430
www.netherlands-embassy.org

New Zealand Embassy
37 Observatory Circle
Washington, D.C. 20008
Tel: 202-328-4800
Fax: 202-667-5227
www.nzemb.org

The Republic of Nicaragua
1627 New Hampshire Avenue NW
Washington, D.C. 20009
Tel: 202-939-6570
Fax: 202-939-6542

The Republic of Niger
2204 R Street NW
Washington, D.C. 20008
Tel: 202-483-4224
Fax: 202-483-3169
www.nigerembassyusa.org

The Federal Republic of Nigeria
1333 16th Street NW
Washington, D.C. 20036
Tel: 202-986-8400
Fax: 202-462-7124
www.nigeriaembassyusa.org

Royal Norwegian Embassy
2720 34th Street NW
Washington, D.C. 20008
Tel: 202-333-6000
Fax: 202-337-0870
www.norway.org

The Sultanate of Oman
2535 Belmont Road NW
Washington, D.C. 20008
Tel: 202-387-1980
Fax: 202-745-4933

The Islamic Republic of Pakistan
3517 International Court
Washington, D.C. 20008
Tel: 202-243-6500
Fax: 202-686-1534
www.embassyofpakistan.com

The Republic of Panama
2862 McGill Terrace NW
Washington, D.C. 20008
Tel: 202-483-1407
Fax: 202-483-8413
www.embassyofpanama.com

Embassy of Papua New Guinea
1779 Massachusetts Avenue NW
Suite 805
Washington, D.C. 20036
Tel: 202-745-3680
Fax: 202-745-3679
www.pngembassy.org

Paraguay
2400 Massachusetts Avenue NW
Washington, D.C. 20008
Tel: 202-483-6960
Fax: 202-234-4508

Embassy of Peru
1700 Massachusetts Avenue NW
Washington, D.C. 20036
Tel: 202-833-9860
Fax: 202-659-8124
www.peruvianembassy.us

Embassy of the Philippines
1600 Massachusetts Avenue NW
Washington, D.C. 20036
Tel: 202-467-9300
Fax: 202-467-9417
www.philippineembassy-usa.org

Embassy of Poland
2640 16th Street NW
Washington, D.C. 20009
Tel: 202-234-3800
Fax: 202-328-6271
www.polandembassy.org

Embassy of Portugal
2125 Kalorama Road NW
Washington, D.C. 20008
Tel: 202-328-8610
Fax: 202-462-3726
www.portugalemb.org

Embassy of The State of Qatar
2555 M Street NW
Washington, D.C. 20037
Tel: 202-274-1600
Fax: 202-237-0061
www.qatarembassy.net

Embassy of Romania
1607 23rd Street NW
Washington, D.C. 20008
Tel: 202-332-4848
Fax: 202-232-4748
www.roembus.org

Embassy of the Russian Federation
2650 Wisconsin Avenue NW
Washington, D.C. 20007
Tel: 202-298-5700
Fax: 202-298-5735
www.russianembassy.org

The Republic of Rwanda
1714 New Hampshire Avenue NW
Washington, D.C. 20009
Tel: 202-232-2882
Fax: 202-232-4544
www.rwandemb.org

Embassy of Saint Kitts and Nevis
3216 New Mexico Avenue NW
Washington, D.C. 20016
Tel: 202-686-2636
Fax: 202-686-5740

Embassy of Saint Lucia
3216 New Mexico Avenue NW
Washington, D.C. 20016
Tel: 202-364-6792 /93 /94 /95
Fax: 202-364-6723

Embassy of Saint Vincent and the Grenadines
3216 New Mexico Avenue NW
Washington, D.C. 20016
Tel: 202-364-6730
Fax: 202-364-6736

Royal Embassy of Saudi Arabia
601 New Hampshire Avenue NW
Washington, D.C. 20037
Tel: 202-342-3800
www.saudiembassy.net

Embassy of the Republic of Senegal
2112 Wyoming Avenue NW
Washington, D.C. 20008
Tel: 202-234-0540
Fax: 202-332-6315
www.senegalembassy-us.org

Embassy of Serbia and Montenegro
2134 Kalorama Road NW
Washington, D.C. 20008
Tel: 202-332-0333
Fax: 202-332-3933
www.serbiaembusa.org

Embassy of Sierra Leone
1701 19th Street NW
Washington, D.C. 20009
Tel: 202-939-9261
Fax: 202-483-1793

The Republic of Singapore
3501 International Place NW
Washington, D.C. 20008
Tel: 202-537-3100
Fax: 202-537-0876

Embassy of the Slovak Republic
3523 International Court NW
Washington, D.C. 20008
Tel: 202-237-1054
Fax: 202-237-6438
www.slovakembassy-us.org

Embassy of the Republic of Slovenia
1525 New Hampshire Avenue NW
Washington, D.C. 20036
Tel: 202-667-5363
Fax: 202-667-4563
www.mzz.gov.si/index.php?id=6&L=2

South African Embassy
3051 Massachusetts Avenue NW
Washington, D.C. 20008
Tel: 202-232-4400
Fax: 202-265-1607
www.saembassy.org

Embassy of Spain
2375 Pennsylvania Avenue NW
Washington, D.C. 20037
Tel: 202-452-0100
Fax: 202-833-5670
www.mae.es/en/home

Sri Lanka
2148 Wyoming Avenue NW
Washington, D.C. 20008
Tel: 202-483-4025 /26 /27 /28
Fax: 202-232-7181
www.slembassyusa.org

Embassy of the Republic of the Sudan
2210 Massachusetts Avenue NW
Washington, D.C. 20008
Tel: 202-338-8565
Fax: 202-667-2406
www.sudanembassy.org

Embassy of the Republic of Suriname
4301 Connecticut Avenue NW
Suite 460
Washington, D.C. 20008
Tel: 202-244-7488
Fax: 202-244-5878

Embassy of the Kingdom of Swaziland
3400 International Drive NW
Washington, D.C. 20008

Embassy of Sweden
2900 K Street
Washington, D.C. 20007
Tel: 202-467-2600
Fax: 202-467-2656
www.swedenabroad.se

Embassy of Switzerland
2900 Cathedral Avenue NW
Washington, D.C. 20008
Tel: 202-745-7900
Fax: 202-387-2564
www.swissemb.org

The Syrian Arab Republic
2215 Wyoming Avenue NW
Washington, D.C. 20008
Tel: 202-232-6313
Fax: 202-234-9548

The Republic of China on Taiwan
4201 Wisconsin Avenue NW
Washington, D.C. 20016
Tel: 202-895-1800
Fax: 202-966-0825

Embassy of Tajikistan
1005 New Hampshire Avenue NW
Washington, D.C. 20037
Tel: 202-223-6090
Fax: 202-223-6091
www.tjus.org

The United Republic of Tanzania
2139 R Street NW
Washington, D.C. 20008
Tel: 202-939-6125
Fax: 202-797-7408
www.tanzaniaembassy-us.org

Royal Thai Embassy
1024 Wisconsin Avenue NW
Suite 401
Washington, D.C. 20007
Tel: 202-944-3600
Fax: 202-944-3611
www.thaiembdc.org

The Republic of Togo
2208 Massachusetts Avenue NW
Washington, D.C. 20008
Tel: 202-234-4212
Fax: 202-232-3190

The Republic of Trinidad and Tobago
1708 Massachusetts Avenue NW
Washington, D.C. 20036
Tel: 202-467-6490
Fax: 202-785-3130
www.ttembassy.cjb.net

Tunisia
1515 Massachusetts Avenue NW
Washington, D.C. 20005
Tel: 202-862-1850
Fax: 202-862-1858

Embassy of the Republic of Turkey
2525 Massachusetts Avenue NW
Washington, D.C. 20008
Tel: 202-612-6700
Fax: 202-612-6744
www.turkishembassy.org

Embassy of Uganda
5911 16th Street NW
Washington, D.C. 20011
Tel: 202-726-7100
Fax: 202-726-1727
www.ugandaembassy.us

Embassy of Ukraine
3350 M Street NW
Washington, D.C. 20007
Tel: 202-333-0606
Fax: 202-333-0817
www.ukraineinfo.us

The United Arab Emirates
3522 International Court NW
Suite 400
Washington, D.C. 20008
Tel: 202-243-2400
Fax: 202-243-2432

**The United Kingdom of Great Britain and
  Northern Ireland**
3100 Massachusetts Avenue NW
Washington, D.C. 20006
Tel: 202-588-6500
Fax: 202-588-7870
www.britainusa.com/embassy

Embassy of Uruguay
1913 I Street NW
Washington D.C. 20006
Tel: 202-331-1313
Fax: 202-331-8142
www.uruwashi.org

Embassy of the Republic of Uzbekistan
1746 Massachusetts Avenue NW
Washington, D.C. 20036
Tel: 202-887-5300
Fax: 202-293-6804
www.uzbekistan.org

The Embassy of Venezuela
1099 30th Street NW
Washington, D.C. 20007
Tel: 202-342-2214
Fax: 202-342-6820
www.embavenez-us.org

The Embassy of Vietnam
1233 20th Street NW
Suite 400
Washington, D.C. 20037
Tel: 202-861-0737
Fax: 202-861-0917
www.vietnamembassy-usa.org

Embassy of the Independent State of Samoa
800 2nd Avenue
Suite 400D
New York, NY 10017
Tel: 212-599-6196
Fax: 212-599-0797

Embassy of Yemen
2319 Wyoming Avenue NW
Washington, D.C. 20037
Tel: 202-965-4760
Fax: 202-337-2017
www.yemenembassy.org

The Republic of Zambia
2419 Massachusetts Avenue NW
Washington, D.C. 20008
Tel: 202-265-9717
Fax: 202-332-0826

The Republic of Zimbabwe
1608 New Hampshire Avenue NW
Washington, D.C. 20009
Tel: 202-332-7100
Fax: 202-483-9326

APÉNDICE B

✪ Recursos en tu comunidad

Asian-American Community Service Association
11322-F East 21st Street
Tulsa, OK 74129
Tel: 918-234-7431
Fax: 918-234-3148

Ayuda, Inc.
1707 Kalorama Road NW
Washington, D.C. 20009
Tel: 202-387-4848
Fax: 202-387-0324
www.ayudainc.org

American Immigration Lawyers Association
918 F Street NW
Washington, D.C. 20004-1400
Tel: 202-216-2400
Fax: 202-783-7853
www.aila.org

Catholic Charities USA
1731 King Street
Alexandria, VA 22314
Tel: 703-549-1390
Fax: 703-549-1656
www.catholiccharitiesusa.org

Colombian American Service Association (C.A.S.A.)
8500 SW 8 Street
Suite 218
Miami, FL 33144
Tel: 305-448-2272
Fax: 305-448-0178
www.casa-usa.org

Emerald Isle Immigration Center
Queens Office
59-26 Woodside Avenue
Woodside, NY 11377
Tel: 718-478-5502
Fax: 718-446-3727
www.eiic.org

Bronx Office
280 East 236th Street
Woodlawn, NY 10470
Tel: 718-324-3039
Fax: 718-324-7741
www.eiic.org

Ethiopian Community Development Council, Inc.
901 South Highland Street
Arlington, VA 22204
Tel: 703-685-0510
Fax: 703-685-0529
www.ecdcinternational.org

The Hebrew Immigrant Aid Society
333 7th Avenue, 16th Floor
New York, NY 10001-5004
Tel: 212-967-4100
Fax: 212-967-4483
www.hias.org

Indo-American Center
6328 North California Avenue
Chicago, IL 60659
Tel: 773-973-4444
Fax: 773-973-0157
www.indoamerican.org

Korean American Coalition
3727 West 6th Street, Suite 515
Los Angeles, CA 90020
Tel: 213-365-5999
Fax: 213-380-7990
www.kacla.org

League of United Latin American Citizens Foundation (LULAC)
2000 L Street NW
Suite 610
Washington, D.C. 20036
Tel: 202-833-6130
Fax: 202-833-6135
www.lulac.org

Los Angeles Unified School District
Division of Adult and Career Education
2333 South Beaudry Avenue
Los Angeles, CA 90017
Tel: 213-241-1000
www.lausd.k12.ca.us

Lutheran Immigration and Refugee Service
National Headquarters
700 Light Street
Baltimore, MD 21230
Tel: 410-230-2700
Fax: 410-230-2890
www.lirs.org

Maryland Office for New Americans (MONA)
Department of Human Resources
311 West Saratoga Street
Baltimore, MD 21201
Tel: 410-767-7514
www.dhr.state.md.us/mona.htm

The Commonwealth of Massachusetts Office for Refugees and Immigrants
1 Ashburton Place
11th Floor
Boston, MA 02108
Tel: 617-573-1600
www.state.ma.us/ori/

New York Association for New Americans, Inc.
17 Battery Place
New York, NY 10004-1102
Tel. 212-425-2900
www.nyana.org

Services, Immigrant Rights, and Education Network (SIREN)
1425 Koll Circle
Suite 103
San Jose, CA 95112
Tel: 408-408-453-3003
Vietnamese Q&A: 408-286-1448
Spanish Info Line: 408-453-3017
www.siren-bayarea.org

St. Anselm's Cross-Cultural Community Center
13091 Galway Street
Garden Grove, CA 92844
Tel: 714-537-0604
Fax: 714-537-7606
www.saintanselmgg.org

Office of Migration & Refugee Services
United States Conference of Catholic Bishops
3211 4th Street NE
Washington, D.C. 20017-1194
Tel: 202-541-3000
www.nccbuscc.org

APÉNDICE C

EJEMPLO DE LA SOLICITUD DEL N-400

N-400 Application
for Naturalization

Department of Homeland Security
U.S Citizenship and Immigration Services

Print clearly or type your answers using CAPITAL letters. Failure to print clearly may delay your application. Use black ink.

Part 1. Your Name. *(The person applying for naturalization.)*

Write your USCIS "A"- number here:
A

A. Your current legal name.

Family Name *(Last Name)*

Given Name *(First Name)*

Full Middle Name *(If applicable)*

For USCIS Use Only

Bar Code	Date Stamp
	Remarks

B. Your name **exactly** as it appears on your Permanent Resident Card.

Family Name *(Last Name)*

Given Name *(First Name)*

Full Middle Name *(If applicable)*

C. If you have ever used other names, provide them below.

Family Name *(Last Name)*	Given Name *(First Name)*	Middle Name

D. Name change *(optional)*

Please read the Instructions before you decide whether to change your name.

1. Would you like to legally change your name? ☐ Yes ☐ No

2. If "Yes," print the new name you would like to use. Do not use initials or abbreviations when writing your new name.

Family Name *(Last Name)*

Given Name *(First Name)*

Full Middle Name

Action Block

Part 2. Information about your eligibility. *(Check only one.)*

I am at least 18 years old **AND**

A. ☐ I have been a Lawful Permanent Resident of the United States for at least five years.

B. ☐ I have been a Lawful Permanent Resident of the United States for at least three years, **and** I have been married to and living with the same U.S. citizen for the last three years, **and** my spouse has been a U.S. citizen for the last three years.

C. ☐ I am applying on the basis of qualifying military service.

D. ☐ Other *(Please explain)* _____

A. U.S. Social Security Number

B. Date of Birth *(mm/dd/yyyy)*

C. Date You Became a Permanent Resident *(mm/dd/yyyy)*

D. Country of Birth

E. Country of Nationality

F. Are either of your parents U.S. citizens? *(If yes, see instructions.)* ☐ Yes ☐ No

G. What is your current marital status? ☐ Single, Never Married ☐ Married ☐ Divorced ☐ Widowed

☐ Marriage Annulled or Other *(Explain)* _____

H. Are you requesting a waiver of the English and/or U.S. History and Government requirements based on a disability or impairment and attaching a Form N-648 with your application? ☐ Yes ☐ No

I. Are you requesting an accommodation to the naturalization process because of a disability or impairment? *(See Instructions for some examples of accommodations.)* ☐ Yes ☐ No

If you answered "Yes," check the box below that applies:

☐ I am deaf or hearing impaired and need a sign language interpreter who uses the following language: _____

☐ I use a wheelchair.

☐ I am blind or sight impaired.

☐ I will need another type of accommodation. Please explain: _____

_____

_____

Part 4. Addresses and telephone numbers.

A. Home Address - Street Number and Name *(Do **not** write a P.O. Box in this space.)*

Apartment Number

City | County | State | ZIP Code | Country

B. Care of

Mailing Address - Street Number and Name *(If different from home address)*

Apartment Number

City | State | ZIP Code | Country

C. Daytime Phone Number *(If any)* (   )

Evening Phone Number *(If any)* (   )

E-mail Address *(If any)*

NOTE: The categories below are those required by the FBI. See Instructions for more information.

A. Gender

☐ Male ☐ Female

B. Height

Feet	Inches

C. Weight

Pounds

D. Are you Hispanic or Latino?   ☐ Yes   ☐ No

E. Race *(Select one or more.)*

☐ White   ☐ Asian   ☐ Black or African American   ☐ American Indian or Alaskan Native   ☐ Native Hawaiian or Other Pacific Islander

F. Hair color

☐ Black   ☐ Brown   ☐ Blonde   ☐ Gray   ☐ White   ☐ Red   ☐ Sandy   ☐ Bald (No Hair)

G. Eye color

☐ Brown   ☐ Blue   ☐ Green   ☐ Hazel   ☐ Gray   ☐ Black   ☐ Pink   ☐ Maroon   ☐ Other

Part 6. Information about your residence and employment.

A. Where have you lived during the last five years? Begin with where you live now and then list every place you lived for the last five years. If you need more space, use a separate sheet(s) of paper.

Street Number and Name, Apartment Number, City, State, Zip Code and Country	Dates *(mm/dd/yyyy)*	
	From	To
Current Home Address - Same as Part 4.A		Present

B. Where have you worked (or, if you were a student, what schools did you attend) during the last five years? Include military service. Begin with your current or latest employer and then list every place you have worked or studied for the last five years. If you need more space, use a separate sheet of paper.

Employer or School Name	Employer or School Address *(Street, City and State)*	Dates *(mm/dd/yyyy)*		Your Occupation
		From	To	

A. How many total days did you spend outside of the United States during the past five years? ☐ days

B. How many trips of 24 hours or more have you taken outside of the United States during the past five years? ☐ trips

C. List below all the trips of 24 hours or more that you have taken outside of the United States since becoming a Lawful Permanent Resident. Begin with your most recent trip. If you need more space, use a separate sheet(s) of paper.

Date You Left the United States *(mm/dd/yyyy)*	Date You Returned to the United States *(mm/dd/yyyy)*	Did Trip Last Six Months or More?	Countries to Which You Traveled	Total Days Out of the United States
		☐ Yes ☐ No		
		☐ Yes ☐ No		
		☐ Yes ☐ No		
		☐ Yes ☐ No		
		☐ Yes ☐ No		
		☐ Yes ☐ No		
		☐ Yes ☐ No		
		☐ Yes ☐ No		
		☐ Yes ☐ No		
		☐ Yes ☐ No		

Part 8. Information about your marital history.

A. How many times have you been married (including annulled marriages)? ☐ If you have **never** been married, go to Part 9.

B. If you are now married, give the following information about your spouse:

1. Spouse's Family Name *(Last Name)*   Given Name *(First Name)*   Full Middle Name *(If applicable)*

2. Date of Birth *(mm/dd/yyyy)*   **3.** Date of Marriage *(mm/dd/yyyy)*   **4.** Spouse's U.S. Social Security #

5. Home Address - Street Number and Name   Apartment Number

City   State   Zip Code

C. Is your spouse a U.S. citizen? ☐ Yes ☐ No

D. If your spouse is a U.S. citizen, give the following information:

   1. When did your spouse become a U.S. citizen? ☐ At Birth ☐ Other

     If "Other," give the following information:

   2. Date your spouse became a U.S. citizen

   3. Place your spouse became a U.S. citizen *(Please see Instructions.)*

     City and State

E. If your spouse is **not** a U.S. citizen, give the following information :

   1. Spouse's Country of Citizenship

   2. Spouse's USCIS "A"- Number *(If applicable)*
     A

   3. Spouse's Immigration Status

     ☐ Lawful Permanent Resident   ☐ Other

F. If you were married before, provide the following information about your prior spouse. If you have more than one previous marriage, use a separate sheet(s) of paper to provide the information requested in Questions 1-5 below.

   1. Prior Spouse's Family Name *(Last Name)*   Given Name *(First Name)*   Full Middle Name *(If applicable)*

   2. Prior Spouse's Immigration Status

     ☐ U.S. Citizen

     ☐ Lawful Permanent Resident

     ☐ Other

   3. Date of Marriage *(mm/dd/yyyy)*

   4. Date Marriage Ended *(mm/dd/yyyy)*

   5. How Marriage Ended

     ☐ Divorce ☐ Spouse Died ☐ Other

G. How many times has your current spouse been married (including annulled marriages)?

   If your spouse has **ever** been married before, give the following information about **your spouse's** prior marriage.
   If your spouse has more than one previous marriage, use a separate sheet(s) of paper to provide the information requested in Questions 1 - 5 below.

   1. Prior Spouse's Family Name *(Last Name)*   Given Name *(First Name)*   Full Middle Name *(If applicable)*

   2. Prior Spouse's Immigration Status

     ☐ U.S. Citizen

     ☐ Lawful Permanent Resident

     ☐ Other

   3. Date of Marriage *(mm/dd/yyyy)*

   4. Date Marriage Ended *(mm/dd/yyyy)*

   5. How Marriage Ended

     ☐ Divorce ☐ Spouse Died ☐ Other

Part 9. Information about your children.	Write your USCIS "A"- number here: A

A. How many sons and daughters have you had? For more information on which sons and daughters you should include and how to complete this section, see the Instructions.

B. Provide the following information about all of your sons and daughters. If you need more space, use a separate sheet(s) of paper.

Full Name of Son or Daughter	Date of Birth (mm/dd/yyyy)	USCIS "A"- number (if child has one)	Country of Birth	Current Address (Street, City, State and Country)
		A		
		A		
		A		
		A		
		A		
		A		
		A		
		A		

Add Children	Go to continuation page

Part 10. Additional questions.

Please answer Questions 1 through 14. If you answer "Yes" to any of these questions, include a written explanation with this form. Your written explanation should (1) explain why your answer was "Yes" and (2) provide any additional information that helps to explain your answer.

A. General Questions.

1. Have you **ever** claimed to be a U.S. citizen *(in writing or any other way)*? ☐ Yes ☐ No

2. Have you **ever** registered to vote in any Federal, state or local election in the United States? ☐ Yes ☐ No

3. Have you **ever** voted in any Federal, state or local election in the United States? ☐ Yes ☐ No

4. Since becoming a Lawful Permanent Resident, have you **ever** failed to file a required Federal state or local tax return? ☐ Yes ☐ No

5. Do you owe any Federal, state or local taxes that are overdue? ☐ Yes ☐ No

6. Do you have any title of nobility in any foreign country? ☐ Yes ☐ No

7. Have you ever been declared legally incompetent or been confined to a mental institution within the last five years? ☐ Yes ☐ No

B. Affiliations.

8. a Have you **ever** been a member of or associated with any organization, association, fund foundation, party, club, society or similar group in the United States or in any other place?   ☐ Yes ☐ No

b. If you answered "Yes," list the name of each group below. If you need more space, attach the names of the other group(s) on a separate sheet(s) of paper.

Name of Group	Name of Group
1.	6.
2.	7.
3.	8.
4.	9.
5.	10.

9. Have you **ever** been a member of or in any way associated *(either directly or indirectly)* with:

   a. The Communist Party?   ☐ Yes ☐ No

   b. Any other totalitarian party?   ☐ Yes ☐ No

   c. A terrorist organization?   ☐ Yes ☐ No

10. Have you **ever** advocated *(either directly or indirectly)* the overthrow of any government by force or violence?   ☐ Yes ☐ No

11. Have you **ever** persecuted *(either directly or indirectly)* any person because of race, religion, national origin, membership in a particular social group or political opinion?   ☐ Yes ☐ No

12. Between March 23, 1933 and May 8, 1945, did you work for or associate in any way *(either directly or indirectly)* with:

   a. The Nazi government of Germany?   ☐ Yes ☐ No

   b. Any government in any area (1) occupied by, (2) allied with, or (3) established with the help of the Nazi government of Germany?   ☐ Yes ☐ No

   c. Any German, Nazi, or S.S. military unit, paramilitary unit, self-defense unit, vigilante unit, citizen unit, police unit, government agency or office, extermination camp, concentration camp, prisoner of war camp, prison, labor camp or transit camp?   ☐ Yes ☐ No

C. Continuous Residence.

Since becoming a Lawful Permanent Resident of the United States:

13. Have you **ever** called yourself a "nonresident" on a Federal, state or local tax return?   ☐ Yes ☐ No

14. Have you **ever** failed to file a Federal, state or local tax return because you considered yourself to be a "nonresident"?   ☐ Yes ☐ No

D. Good Moral Character.

For the purposes of this application, you must answer "Yes" to the following questions, if applicable, even if your records were sealed or otherwise cleared or if anyone, including a judge, law enforcement officer or attorney, told you that you no longer have a record.

15. Have you **ever** committed a crime or offense for which you were **not** arrested? ☐ Yes ☐ No

16. Have you **ever** been arrested, cited or detained by any law enforcement officer (including USCIS or former INS and military officers) for any reason? ☐ Yes ☐ No

17. Have you **ever** been charged with committing any crime or offense? ☐ Yes ☐ No

18. Have you **ever** been convicted of a crime or offense? ☐ Yes ☐ No

19. Have you **ever** been placed in an alternative sentencing or a rehabilitative program (for example: diversion, deferred prosecution, withheld adjudication, deferred adjudication)? ☐ Yes ☐ No

20. Have you **ever** received a suspended sentence, been placed on probation or been paroled? ☐ Yes ☐ No

21. Have you **ever** been in jail or prison? ☐ Yes ☐ No

If you answered "Yes" to any of Questions 15 through 21, complete the following table. If you need more space, use a separate sheet (s) of paper to give the same information.

Why were you arrested, cited, detained or charged?	Date arrested, cited, detained or charged? *(mm/dd/yyyy)*	Where were you arrested, cited, detained or charged? *(City, State, Country)*	Outcome or disposition of the arrest, citation, detention or charge *(No charges filed, charges dismissed, jail, probation, etc.)*

Answer Questions 22 through 33. If you answer "Yes" to any of these questions, attach (1) your written explanation why your answer was "Yes" and (2) any additional information or documentation that helps explain your answer.

22. Have you **ever:**

    a. Been a habitual drunkard? ☐ Yes ☐ No

    b. Been a prostitute, or procured anyone for prostitution? ☐ Yes ☐ No

    c. Sold or smuggled controlled substances, illegal drugs or narcotics? ☐ Yes ☐ No

    d. Been married to more than one person at the same time? ☐ Yes ☐ No

    e. Helped anyone enter or try to enter the United States illegally? ☐ Yes ☐ No

    f. Gambled illegally or received income from illegal gambling? ☐ Yes ☐ No

    g. Failed to support your dependents or to pay alimony? ☐ Yes ☐ No

23. Have you **ever** given false or misleading information to any U.S. government official while applying for any immigration benefit or to prevent deportation, exclusion or removal? ☐ Yes ☐ No

24. Have you **ever** lied to any U.S. government official to gain entry or admission into the United States? ☐ Yes ☐ No

E. Removal, Exclusion and Deportation Proceedings.

25. Are removal, exclusion, rescission or deportation proceedings pending against you? ☐ Yes ☐ No

26. Have you **ever** been removed, excluded or deported from the United States? ☐ Yes ☐ No

27. Have you **ever** been ordered to be removed, excluded or deported from the United States? ☐ Yes ☐ No

28. Have you **ever** applied for any kind of relief from removal, exclusion or deportation? ☐ Yes ☐ No

F. Military Service.

29. Have you **ever** served in the U.S. Armed Forces? ☐ Yes ☐ No

30. Have you **ever** left the United States to avoid being drafted into the U.S. Armed Forces? ☐ Yes ☐ No

31. Have you **ever** applied for any kind of exemption from military service in the U.S. Armed Forces? ☐ Yes ☐ No

32. Have you **ever** deserted from the U.S. Armed Forces? ☐ Yes ☐ No

G. Selective Service Registration.

33. Are you a male who lived in the United States at any time between your 18th and 26th birthdays in any status except as a lawful nonimmigrant? ☐ Yes ☐ No

If you answered "NO," go on to question 34.

If you answered "YES," provide the information below.

If you answered "YES," but you did not register with the Selective Service System and are still under 26 years of age, you must register before you apply for naturalization, so that you can complete the information below:

Date Registered (mm/dd/yyyy) [   ]   Selective Service Number [   ]

If you answered "YES," but you did not register with the Selective Service and you are now 26 years old or older, attach a statement explaining why you did not register.

H. Oath Requirements. *(See Part 14 for the Text of the Oath.)*

Answer Questions 34 through 39. If you answer "No" to any of these questions, attach (1) your written explanation why the answer was "No" and (2) any additional information or documentation that helps to explain your answer.

34. Do you support the Constitution and form of government of the United States? ☐ Yes ☐ No

35. Do you understand the full Oath of Allegiance to the United States? ☐ Yes ☐ No

36. Are you willing to take the full Oath of Allegiance to the United States? ☐ Yes ☐ No

37. If the law requires it, are you willing to bear arms on behalf of the United States? ☐ Yes ☐ No

38. If the law requires it, are you willing to perform noncombatant services in the U.S. Armed Forces? ☐ Yes ☐ No

39. If the law requires it, are you willing to perform work of national importance under civilian direction? ☐ Yes ☐ No

Part 11. Your signature.

Write your USCIS "A"- number here:
A

I certify, under penalty of perjury under the laws of the United States of America, that this application, and the evidence submitted with it, are all true and correct. I authorize the release of any information that the USCIS needs to determine my eligibility for naturalization.

Your Signature

Date (mm/dd/yyyy)

Part 12. Signature of person who prepared this application for you. *(If applicable.)*

I declare under penalty of perjury that I prepared this application at the request of the above person. The answers provided are based on information of which I have personal knowledge and/or were provided to me by the above named person in response to the *exact questions* contained on this form.

Preparer's Printed Name

Preparer's Signature

Date (mm/dd/yyyy)

Preparer's Firm or Organization Name *(If applicable)*

Preparer's Daytime Phone Number

Preparer's Address - Street Number and Name

City

State

Zip Code

NOTE: Do not complete Parts 13 and 14 until a USCIS Officer instructs you to do so.

Part 13. Signature at interview.

I swear (affirm) and certify under penalty of perjury under the laws of the United States of America that I know that the contents of this application for naturalization subscribed by me, including corrections numbered 1 through _____ and the evidence submitted by me numbered pages 1 through _____ , are true and correct to the best of my knowledge and belief.

Subscribed to and sworn to (affirmed) before me

Officer's Printed Name or Stamp

Date (mm/dd/yyyy)

Complete Signature of Applicant

Officer's Signature

Part 14. Oath of Allegiance.

If your application is approved, you will be scheduled for a public oath ceremony at which time you will be required to take the following oath of allegiance immediately prior to becoming a naturalized citizen. By signing, you acknowledge your willingness and ability to take this oath:

I hereby declare, on oath, that I absolutely and entirely renounce and abjure all allegiance and fidelity to any foreign prince, potentate, state, or sovereignty, of whom or which I have heretofore been a subject or citizen;

that I will support and defend the Constitution and laws of the United States of America against all enemies, foreign and domestic;

that I will bear true faith and allegiance to the same;

that I will bear arms on behalf of the United States when required by the law;

that I will perform noncombatant service in the Armed Forces of the United States when required by the law;

that I will perform work of national importance under civilian direction when required by the law; and

that I take this obligation freely, without any mental reservation or purpose of evasion; so help me God.

Printed Name of Applicant

Complete Signature of Applicant